THE JESUS YOU NEED TO KNOW

HOW JESUS, EPICURUS, AND THE MODERN SCIENCE OF HAPPINESS CAN CHANGE YOUR LIFE

R. EARLE RABB

Printed by R. Earle Rabb in the United States

First printing, 2021.

ISBN: 978-1-7358164-9-4

*For my fourteen grandchildren and
all the grandchildren of the world,
with the belief they will know that
generous sharing of Love and Happiness
with others makes the world a better
place for everyone.*

TABLE OF CONTENTS

ACKNOWLEDGEMENTS

There are many people who have made possible the journey this book represents. These include my colleagues, teachers, professors, parishioners, friends, and many others who through the years have enriched my life and without whom this book could not have been written.

My heartfelt thanks to David Alf, Denis Bolena, Matt Cannizzio, Dan Carter, Alice Hardy, Ernie Mills, Peter Mockridge, Don O'Dell, and Bill Thomas, who read a late draft of this book. Their tactful responses helped make this a much better book.

I am indebted to many from whose books, articles, and lectures I have learned, but two deserve special mention, for their work has been particularly influential on this book: the scholars I have met through the Jesus Seminar who have deepened my thinking and challenged my mind on many occasions and the researchers in the Science of Happiness, whose work added depth to Part Five of this book.

Words cannot adequately express the enormous gratitude I feel toward my editor, Jim Hardy, for the countless hours he spent reading and rereading each successive draft and discussing with me his suggestions for improving this book. From the original concept to the final draft, Jim's encouragement and wise counsel supported and guided me to produce the work you now hold.

I would particularly like to acknowledge my wife, Ann, who has always been an inexhaustible source of advice, strength, and encouragement. I am grateful for her ongoing support and her willingness to put up with my prolonged periods ensconced at my computer. I will always be indebted to her for her continual patience and understanding.

Finally, I want to thank you, the reader, for your inquisitive mind and your willingness to explore the new possibilities offered through the wisdom of Epicurus, Jesus, and the Science of Wellbeing and Happiness.

1

FOREWORD

Wisdom comes to the inquisitive mind.

Anonymous

My formal journey toward my 43-year career as a United Methodist minister began at Drew University School of Theology in 1961. There I learned I could take the Bible seriously without taking it literally. That freed me to study the Bible with honesty and integrity. In the process, my Christian faith grew and expanded as I gained deeper insights into what it means to be a Christian. In my study of the four New Testament gospels, I learned to identify the words of Jesus and to separate them from the words attributed to him by the writers of the gospels. As I studied the words spoken by Jesus himself, I came to see his wisdom as a guide for living an abundant and fulfilling life. Through this process Jesus became a mentor for me. My personal faith and beliefs became more real. I also realized this same experience could be available to those to whom I ministered, and I could provide a vehicle for the members of my congregations to grow and expand their understanding of what it means to be a Christian follower of Jesus.

Later in my ministry I also became familiar with the philosophy of the ancient Greek philosopher Epicurus. As I studied his life and teachings, I began to see numerous parallels between his teachings and those of Jesus. I realized these teachings offer profound and practical wisdom for living our individual and societal lives together. As a result of this discovery, I bring this book to you.

In my prior book, *The Case of the Missing Person,* I focused on the social dimension of the teachings of Jesus. He followed in the footsteps of the social prophets of Israel by emphasizing the importance of the social dimension of the community. He built on the traditional Hebrew wisdom that individual lives are shaped by the community in which they live. If you want to produce healthy and wholesome individuals, you start by producing healthy and wholesome communities on the local, state, national, and global levels. Community comes first and individuals follow.

I followed that concept by first writing about Jesus as a visionary sage, social prophet, and community builder. Now I will focus on Jesus' concern for individual happiness and well-being. I also bring Epicurus into the picture, thus providing both a philosophical and religious foundation to this book. Regardless of one's religious beliefs or lack of them, the combined wisdom of these two ancient teachers provides a path to happiness and fulfillment.

The primary connection between Epicurus and Jesus is that they believed humans have the potential to flourish. Both pragmatists, they spent their adult years teaching humanity how to live meaningful and happy lives. Everyone wants to be happy, to have a life with a sense of purpose and meaning. Yet, despite our desire to achieve it, a happy and meaningful life often eludes us. Their message provides a clear path to that elusive goal. The Gospel of John had it right: Jesus came that we "may have life and have it more abundantly."

At first glance it may seem that happiness is a trivial, selfish goal. In fact, it is not, and modern research has proven what Jesus and Epicurus knew and taught: happy people are productive, compassionate, generous, thoughtful, and ethical in comparison to those who are unhappy. Happy people are better neighbors, companions, friends, and citizens than those who are not. People who are happy care about other people and work to make life better for those in their community. They understand that happy people foster a happy community, which makes life better for everyone.

My goal is to reveal the surprising connection between Epicurus and Jesus, explore their combined wisdom, a wisdom that often has been overlooked and lost by those who worship in Jesus' name, and examine how their teaching can enhance not only our individual lives, but also our national and global lives together.

*****

This book is written for a general audience. Therefore, I have refrained from using footnotes which, while being of interest to academic scholars, would bog down the general reader with numerous unnecessary details. I do acknowledge, however, that the scholarly works of many authors have made it possible for me to put together the contents of this book. I am deeply indebted to each one, and I hope the listing of their works in the bibliography will serve as an expression of my gratitude for their scholarly work and a source of further study for the reader.

The Bible translation I will use most often is the 1989 New Revised Standard Version (NRSV). This version has been compiled by biblical scholars, is written in contemporary English, and is based upon the most recent knowledge in biblical studies. On occasion, I will also use The Five Gospels, a contemporary version of the gospels, edited by The Jesus Seminar.

When I refer to historical dates, I will use the letters BCE or CE. The letters follow the commonly accepted practice of dating the modern calendar from the date of Jesus' birth. The dates prior to his birth are indicated by the letters BCE (Before the Common Era), while the dates after Jesus' birth are noted by the letters CE (Common Era).

PREFACE

Happiness. It is something we all want, and we spend our lives in search of it. What is it, and why is it so important to us? Despite our desire to achieve it, it often eludes us.

So, what is the secret of true happiness? Actually, the answer to that question has been with us for over 2000 years and is readily available to anyone who looks for it. Two men who lived 300 years apart spent their lives teaching it to those around them, and both gained considerable notoriety. The purpose of this book is to rediscover these two men and their real message, their vision.

The first to articulate the secret to true wellbeing and happiness was a Greek philosopher who lived around 300 BCE. His name was Epicurus, and his philosophy became so popular it was the dominant philosophy throughout the known Western world for seven centuries after his death.

The second was Jesus of Nazareth, and his impact upon our world is clear. Today, 2,200,000,000 people, almost one third of the earth's population, call themselves Christians. They worship a Jesus whose message and vision were shaped by others after his death, for reasons that had little to do with, in fact were often the exact opposite, of what Jesus taught.

In the 2000 years following the death of Jesus, the primary message of Christianity has been founded on the following key points:

- Jesus is the son of God and therefore divine.
- He came to earth from Heaven to speak for God and thus save the world and each person in it.
- His death on the cross was a sacrificial act, done to atone for the sins of humanity.

5

- The only path to a glorious eternal life in Heaven is by accepting and believing the above. Failure to do so means exclusion from Heaven, which results in various negative consequences, the specifics of which depend on the individual brand of Christianity.

- The vision described above is the one Universal Truth. Those who follow it are the righteous and the saved; those who do not are the wicked and the damned.

Through the centuries, this vision has dominated Western thought and action, often with disastrous results.

Was this the vision Jesus intended when he spoke to the multitudes and traveled throughout Galilee? Did he intend to divide the world as described above into the saved and the damned with the disastrous results we have seen?

I believe the answer to both questions is a resounding No! Based on a close examination of the latest biblical scholarship, which seeks to identify which of Jesus' words were spoken by him and which were created by others to support their own views, I will show that his message was one of compassion and love for each and every human being. He accepted all as equal and refused to divide people into groups. This is the same basic message that Epicurus shared before him.

I will examine in detail the message of each and show how living according to their vision can bring peace and happiness to all mankind. Sadly, much of that message has been eclipsed by the dominant vision embraced by Christianity for the last 2000 years. I will explain how and why Christianity took a fateful turn and the consequences of that choice. Finally, I will show how Jesus' message of love and compassion can remake our world into a more peaceful and just place based on acceptance and connection, not division.

This book was a pleasure to write, not only because it unites my passion for the combined wisdom of Epicurus and Jesus, but also my interest in the recently developing Science of Well-being and Happiness. It is an exhilarating mix! Ancient wisdom without science prevents us from incorporating new understandings. Science without ancient wisdom prevents us from developing deep understandings.

PEOPLE & EVENTS

Many dates are approximate

	BCE
Plato	c. 427-347
Aristotle	c. 384-322
Epicurus	c. 341-270
Ecclesiastes	c. 250
	CE
Jesus' birth	c. 4 BCE – 0 CE
Jesus' ministry	c. 27-30
Jesus' death	c. 30
Paul's call to ministry	c. 35-36
Paul's writings	c. 50-64
Paul's death	c. 64-67
Rome destroys the Temple at Jerusalem	70
The Gospel of Mark	c. 70-75
The Gospel of Matthew	c. 85-90
The Gospel of Luke	c. 85-90
The Gospel of John	c. 90-110

Rest of the New Testament written	c. 100-150
Constantine declares Christianity as the official religion of the Roman Empire	325
Roman Catholic Crusades	c. 1100's
Roman Catholic Inquisitions	c. 1300's
Catholic and Protestant Conquests of Indigenous populations and lands	c. 1500's ff
Beginning of the Protestant Reformation	1513
Founding of the United States of America as an Epicurean-style nation	c. 1776
Beginning of scientifically based Biblical research and scholarship	c. 1850's
Founding of the Jesus Seminar	1985
Beginnings of the Science of Wellbeing and Happiness	c. 1990's

PART ONE

INTRODUCING EPICURUS

Judging whether life is or is not worth living amounts to answering the fundamental question of philosophy. All the rest...comes afterward.

Albert Camus, French philosopher

Introduction to Part One

In antiquity there were two profound teachers of wisdom who focused their attention on how to live a life that is both fulfilling and meaningful. One was Jesus of Nazareth, the other the Greek philosopher, Epicurus, who lived about 300 years prior to Jesus. Their teachings complement each other and together form a solid foundation for living a good and happy life.

Epicurus is a much-misunderstood philosopher. In his day, and even into our current modern period, he has been accused of being both an atheist and a hedonist. As will become clear in Part One, neither accusation is true.

I will provide an overview of his life and teachings and explain why he was unique among the philosophers of Greece. I will also explore the evidence demonstrating Jesus of Nazareth would have been familiar with the teachings of Epicurus.

9

CHAPTER ONE

A Philosopher Like No Other

Underneath a bright blue morning sky, a diverse group is gathering in the garden of a recently purchased home on the outskirts of Athens. They greet each other warmly, and enthusiastically welcome several new arrivals. The word has begun to spread about the new owner of the home and garden, a young philosopher from the city of Lampsacus, who has moved here with a few followers to establish a new philosophical school. The very composition of the group is evidence this young philosopher is different from the more famous Greek philosophers such as Plato and Aristotle. The sign at the garden's entrance hints at this: STRANGER, YOU DO WELL TO TARRY; HERE OUR HIGHEST GOOD IS PLEASURE.

It is the fourth century BCE, and in Greece, philosophy is reserved for the aristocratic, educated elite. Yet, in this garden, ordinary men were welcome to participate in philosophical learning and discussions. The welcome, moreover, extended beyond ordinary men. Women and slaves were not only invited to participate but, remarkably, were treated as equals. This was unheard of in a culture that viewed women as second-class members of society, too simple-minded to participate in the philosophical discussions of the elitist Forum in central Athens. Slaves, of course, were at the bottom rung of society and would never be welcomed into the traditional philosophical schools.

This young philosopher was roundly criticized for welcoming women into his philosophical school, and the word was going around that he was hosting drunken orgies in his home. Despite these severe attacks on him and his school, he stood his ground, defying his critics. What a refreshing and exciting experience it must have been for both women and slaves, as well as the ordinary men of Athens, to find a place where they were warmly welcomed and treated with respect as equals.

The young man who created such a stir in Athens was Epicurus, and his school established a philosophy, which became the most popular philosophy in antiquity. It wasn't Plato, or Aristotle, or Socrates or any of the other Greek philosophers with the most influence in the Greco-Roman world. It was Epicurus who had the major impact on the people of that era, though he is often overlooked and regularly misunderstood. Even today, people know the name, but most have only a vague idea of what his philosophy really taught.

Epicurus lived during a significant transition period in the history of Greece, and this helped shape both his philosophy and outlook on life. He was born in 341 BCE and was seven when Alexander the Great set off on his conquest of much of the known world of that time. Alexander transformed Greece from a small, self-contained nation into the worldwide culture of the Hellenistic period of Greek expansionism. Alexander's conquests gave the citizens of Greece a new and larger perspective of the world and their place in it. Epicurus grew up during these transformative years and used this larger perspective in developing his philosophy of teaching the people of the world how to live a good and happy life.

His Life

Epicurus grew up in the Greek colony of Samos, an island in the Mediterranean Sea off the coast of what is now Turkey. The young Epicurus was an eager learner. During his teen-age years he attended three different Greek philosophical schools. At the age of eighteen he left the island to fulfill his required two years of military training in Athens.

At age twenty-one Epicurus returned to the home of his parents. For the next ten years he studied philosophy under the tutelage of followers of Democritus and Plato. During these years he developed his own unique style of philosophy. Though his teachers focused on eloquent rhetoric and esoteric concepts, Epicurus rejected this approach to philosophy. He revolted against abstract philosophy by proclaiming, *"Vain is the word of that philosopher by which no malady of mankind is healed."* He rejected the pursuit of knowledge for its own sake, be it philosophy or science. He famously said, *"For just as there is no profit in medicine unless it expels the diseases of the body, so there is none in philosophy either unless it expels the malady of the soul."*

When he was thirty-one, he organized and founded his own philosophical school in the Greek city of Mytilene, a city noted for being an intellectual center. He next traveled to Lampsacus, where he developed friendly relationships with the city's philosophical and political leaders. He became quite successful, winning many disciples, and was regarded as a brilliant thinker and teacher.

Athens, however, was regarded as the intellectual and cultural center of Greece, and Epicurus felt the pull to relocate his philosophical school. In 306 BCE at the age of thirty-five he moved with several of his key followers to Athens, where he purchased a house with a garden on the outskirts of the city. He purposefully avoided becoming a part of the official philosophical Academy and Forum, located in the center of the city. Speculative thought had reached its zenith in the previous generation dominated by Plato and Aristotle. Epicurus had no desire to become enmeshed with the abstract philosophical debates occurring at the Academy and Forum.

In the Garden, as it was known, Epicurus established an amiable community of philosophers who studied together and lived a tranquil and happy life with one another. The Garden of Epicurus became famous in antiquity as a place of wholesome living and companionship, as well as profound philosophical thought.

Over his lifetime, Epicurus never departed from his open, welcoming spirit to everyone. Anyone who wished to join was welcome, and all could share in the common meals and discussion, with each person being regarded as an equal.

Epicurus taught in his Garden community for thirty-seven years until his death in 270 BCE at the age of seventy-two. Through those years his purpose was to answer two practical questions: What is the aim of life? and How can one attain it? He lived the simple life he recommended to all his pupils. He was gentle and friendly and gathered many friends and students over the years.

Epicurus believed he had found the way to a life that is both happy and good, and for the sake of humanity he wanted to share his teachings with the whole world. He taught a way to live with grace and wisdom in this difficult and often ambiguous world in which we live. He believed he was engaged in an endeavor that was fundamentally good and would make a difference in the lives of individuals and communities, and ultimately, the world.

His Legacy

His philosophy was designed to appeal to the ordinary educated person. Epicurus offered a plan of life that was a simple, unambitious way of living.

Epicurus understood the value of the textbook style of writing developed by his contemporary Euclid as being especially useful for the instruction of those whom he hoped to win over to his philosophy. In his textbooks Epicurus developed a plain and orderly system of knowledge that could be easily understood by the largest number of people in the ancient world.

Speaking the truth in love was the Epicurean way of teaching. In fact, it was a specialty of the Epicureans. The teacher was to advance the good of the pupil and was warned against reviling, jeering, or injuring feelings. Following the example of Epicurus himself, the teacher offered the gentlest kind of instruction, characterized by timely suggestion rather than sharp criticism.

Epicurus' goal in his teaching was to teach in a plain and simple style a way for individuals and communities to flourish in their daily living.

After His Death

Epicurus' followers believed he had led humankind to the good and happy life and were eager to share his message with the world. Through their efforts, Epicureanism became the first and only Greek world philosophy. For seven centuries Epicureanism was the most popular and widespread Greek philosophy of antiquity. His disciples revered him as a master teacher and esteemed him with an almost godlike admiration.

Nevertheless, his philosophy that happiness and the good life are found in pleasure was strongly opposed by the early Christian church fathers. Due to its popularity throughout the Roman Empire, Epicureanism was viewed by the Apostle Paul and the early church as the chief rival to Christianity. When Christianity gained control of the Roman Empire in the fourth century CE, the church leaders crushed the Epicurean philosophy ruthlessly. They closed all the Epicurean schools and destroyed their books. Sadly, they were successful. None of Epicurus' books have survived intact. Epicureanism was lost to history for the next 1,000 years. It is only through a handful of his letters to his disciples, a collection of his aphorisms known as the "Vatican Sayings" (so designated because the manuscript was discovered in the Vatican library in 1888), and the writings of several of his noted followers that we have knowledge of his philosophy.

French archeologists in the year 1884 discovered an unusual tribute to Epicurus in the city of Oenoanda in southwestern Turkey. A lengthy inscription summarizing the Epicurean philosophy had been etched into a three-hundred-foot wall of a portico in the marketplace around the year 200 BCE, paid for by the millionaire Diogenes Flavianus. It contained his own version of the teachings of Epicurus, as well as certain doctrines of the teacher verbatim. It is eloquent testimony to the ongoing popularity of Epicureanism in that day.

Mention should be made of one of Epicurus' most ardent and capable admirers, the esteemed Roman poet Titus Lucretius Carus (ca. 99-55 BCE). He wrote a didactic poem, *De rerum natura (On the Nature of Things),* extolling and explaining the philosophy of Epicurus. Each of its

7,400 or so lines are dedicated to highlighting the Epicurean philosophy. The poem is a remarkably convincing description of the way things really are.

Lucretius' poem was hugely popular in the Roman Empire. Published about seventy-five years before Jesus began his ministry, the poem increased the popularity of Epicureanism. It had the effect of setting the prose of the philosophy of Epicurus to lyrical music. In antiquity, Lucretius enjoyed immense literary fame as a poet. Ovid (43 BCE-18 CE) praised the sublime poem, writing that the verses of *De rerum natura* would endure until the end of the world.

CHAPTER TWO

His Philosophy

Epicurus' philosophy was practical, a way of living as opposed to a system of thought. One of his main goals was to give people a pathway toward the acquisition of a serenity and tranquility that forms the foundation for a good life. He believed it was a lifelong process:

> *Let no one be slow to seek wisdom when he is young nor weary in the search for it when he has grown old. For no age is too early or too late for the health of the soul.*

His basic question was, "How does one make the most of one's life?" Since we have only one life, we should make it the best possible life. This does not mean riotous living but rather making wise decisions. Epicurus believed we are what we do, not just what we think or what we intend to do. He defined his philosophy thusly:

> *The daily business of speech and thought is to secure a happy life.*

The Pleasure Principle

Epicurus is perhaps best known for his establishment of the Pleasure Principle. He based his philosophy from his observation of nature that every sentient being seeks to find pleasure and avoid pain. Look at the animal kingdom and you will see this principle carried out over and over. It demonstrates that seeking pleasure and happiness is natural.

This pleasure principle can be clearly seen in the actions of an infant. We like to think of babies as innocent and perfect in nature. The newborn baby is totally egocentric. It seeks only to experience pleasure and avoid pain. When it is hungry, it wants to be fed, even if it is 2:00 a.m. and the parents are exhausted. The infant has no regard for the welfare of the parents and will cry and scream until it gets fed or has its diaper changed. Early on, children master the art of doing anything they can think of to get what they want.

This is not a criticism; it is the natural order of life and is necessary for survival. In fact, the pleasure principle enables all sentient beings to survive. Rather than fight against this impulse, Epicurus taught that one can make the most of life by accepting this basic reality, and he taught helpful and constructive ways to do that.

Epicurus had no doubt that the sensible pursuit of pleasure is the essential ingredient of a good and happy life:

> *Pleasure is our first and kindred good. It is the starting point of every choice and every aversion, and to it we return and make feeling the rule by which to judge every good thing.*

Epicurus was careful to clarify exactly what he meant by "pleasure." In a letter, he wrote:

> *When we say that pleasure is the end and aim of life, we do not mean the pleasures of the prodigal, or the pleasures of sensuality, as we are understood by some, through ignorance, prejudice, or willful misinterpretation. By pleasure we mean the absence of pain in the body and trouble in the soul. It is not an unbroken succession of drinking and revelry, nor the enjoyment of female society, nor feasts of fish and other delicacies of a luxurious table, that make life pleasant; it is a sobering reason which searches out the grounds for every choice and avoids and banishes those vain beliefs through which great turmoil takes possession of the soul.*

Not all pleasures, however, are to be pursued. Epicurus taught:

17

Even though pleasure is our first and native good, for that reason we do not choose every pleasure whatsoever, but ofttimes we pass over many pleasures, when greater discomfort accrues to us as the result of them. While, therefore, all pleasure because it is naturally akin to us, is good, not all pleasure is worthy to be chosen, just as all pain is evil but all pain is not to be shunned.

Clearly, Epicurus promotes a life not of indulgence and excess, but of moderation and balance. Following this guidance leads to happiness for everyone. He encourages us to use our physical senses to immediately determine what brings pleasure and what brings pain and to use that information to guide our future decisions.

Epicurus, of course, was roundly criticized for his emphasis upon the pleasure principle by those who did not understand his view. However, his definition of pleasure as *the absence of pain in the body and turmoil in the soul* clarifies the wisdom of his teachings.

Recent scientific studies of the human brain have confirmed the teachings of Epicurus. In 1991, a powerful new tool was developed that revolutionized the study of the human brain. The functional MRI (fMRI) allows researchers to watch the human brain work in real time, as they observe the degree to which various areas of the brain respond—or don't respond--to stimuli. This is akin to going from trying to figure out how a watch works when we are able to observe only the watch's face to taking off the back cover and observing how the various gears and springs connect to make the hands move. Seeing which areas of the brain light up when we experience pleasure—or emotional or physical pain— enables us to link those areas with the various emotions.

We have also discovered much of the brain chemistry at work. For example, dopamine, serotonin, oxytocin, and endorphins play crucial roles in the reward system of the brain, the part that lights up when we feel good. These chemicals bond to specific receptors in the brain to which opioids also bond. Opioid addiction is a major problem and has spurred many studies about the science of addiction. The conclusions drawn from these studies have much to tell us about the pleasure principle developed 2,300 years ago by Epicurus.

The most important is that our brains have evolved over millions of years to seek those things that make us feel good and to avoid those things that make us feel bad. Dopamine works not only to reward us with warm feelings when we experience something pleasant but also to motivate us to repeat that experience. Whether the experience is a chocolate brownie, a hug, a run in the park, work, or any other experience that makes us feel good, our brain is designed to reward us for the experience and motivate us to repeat it. This process is true for humans and for all the animal kingdom: As Epicurus taught, we are fundamentally designed to seek pleasure and avoid pain. And this concept underlies everything this book is about.

Ethics

Every philosophy of life, whether religious or non-religious, proclaims its own ethical ideals and actions. Epicurus focused on the practical matter of how to live an ethical life that combines happiness with morality. He wrote:

> It is impossible to live a pleasant life without living wisely and well and agreeing neither to harm or be harmed, and it is impossible to live wisely and well and justly without living a pleasant life.

Epicurus took exception to the philosophical view of the time that Fate or Fortune control our lives. He felt this view denies human beings the freedom to make our own choices. The person of wisdom, Epicurus taught, will recognize the limitations of the philosophy of determinism and see the value of belief in human freedom:

> Destiny, which some introduce as sovereign over all things, the wise man laughs to scorn, affirming that certain things happen of necessity, others by chance, and others through our own agency. For he sees that necessity destroys responsibility and

that chance or fortune is inconstant; whereas our own actions are free, and it is to them that praise and blame naturally attach. It was better indeed to accept the legends of the gods than to bow beneath the yoke of destiny which the natural philosophers have imposed.

Along with his emphasis upon free will and the freedom to choose, Epicurus placed great importance on the matter of ethics and living an ethical life.

Wisdom

Epicurus believed wisdom resulted from learning the art of making the best choices in life. He called Wisdom "practical reason" and proclaimed it to be *"the greatest good and the beginning of all the other virtues."* It can guide us toward good and useful pleasures, and away from harmful ones. It may even enable us to endure a present pain for the sake of a better pleasure in the future. This method involves weighing the advantages and disadvantages in every decision and action. Epicurus had this to say about the importance of wisdom:

> *Wisdom is a more precious thing even than philosophy, for from it spring all the other virtues. Wisdom teaches us it is not possible to live happily unless one also lives wisely, and honestly, and justly; and that one cannot live wisely and honestly and justly without also living happily. For these virtues are by nature bound up together with the happy life, and the happy life is inseparable from these virtues.*

Epicurus saw wisdom accumulating over one's lifetime and, as it did, enriching that life. He says,

> *It is not the young man who should be considered fortunate, but the old man who has lived well, because the young man in his prime wanders much by chance, vacillating in his beliefs, while the old man has docked in the harbor, having safeguarded his true happiness.*

Self-Control

The route to self-control lies in recognizing that some desires are natural and necessary (food, for example), others are natural but not necessary, and still others are neither natural nor necessary. The key is to make wise choices regarding which desires we seek to fulfill. As Epicurus wrote,

> To all desires must be applied this question: What will be the result for me if the object of this desire is attained and what if it is not?

Epicurus did not agree with those philosophies that promoted the indiscriminate acceptance of all pleasures. He realized many pleasures are detrimental and should be avoided. The "eat, drink, and be merry, for tomorrow we die" philosophy often leads to disaster, because the person does not die tomorrow, and subsequently lives to experience the consequences of choosing harmful pleasures.

Optimism & Health

Epicurus taught that the wise person would choose to live a simple life. This involves living well within one's financial means, which frees the individual from fretting about the material ups and downs of one's daily existence. Thus, one can face the future optimistically.

According to Epicurus, this way of life is active, not passive, and involves planning ahead. It is not about sitting idly and hoping things will work out for the best, but rather about looking toward the future with optimistic goals and working to achieve them. This concept is founded upon his belief that we have some control over our destiny and are not totally bound by the fates.

Epicurus realized that having hope improved one's mental and physical health and that good health improved one's outlook on life and made the individual happier. He says:

The stable condition of sound health in the flesh and the confident hope of this means the height of pleasure and the best assurance of it for those who are able to figure the problem out.

The problem to be figured out relates to the concept of soul and to one's belief in an afterlife. Epicurus rejected the concept of immortality. If a belief in an afterlife is abandoned, this mortal life becomes the only existence one can have. In short, he advocated for living in the moment, without any thought of getting a greater reward in an afterlife. This life is all we will have, so make the best of it.

We should note that Epicurus uses the terms "health of soul" and "health of mind" in an almost interchangeable manner. His concept of *soul* differed from that of most Greek philosophers. Plato and other philosophers in Greece thought of the soul as independent from the human body. A person's soul, they taught, would be freed at death from imprisonment in the human body, and therefore would live on in an afterlife.

Epicurus taught that body and soul are both corporal. He described the soul of a person as the inner self of thoughts, feelings, and attitudes that define who that person is. We now know those aspects of a human being have their origin in the brain and have no existence apart from the human brain. At death, the human brain ceases to function, and therefore all aspects of the soul (thoughts, feelings, attitudes) cease to function.

Epicurus was eager to offer his philosophy of health and healing to all humankind. It was his intention...

> *to issue the kind of oracle that would benefit all men, even if not a soul should understand him.*

Epicurus describes the beautiful life that emerges from his teachings:

> *Considering this, who can you think to be a better man than he who has right opinions about the gods, who is utterly fearless in*

the face of death, who properly contemplates the goals and limits of life as fixed by Nature, and who understands that Nature has established that the greatest goods are readily experienced and easily obtained, while the greatest evils last but a short period and cause only brief pain?

SUMMARY

To achieve a life of happiness, Epicurus advises people to:

Meditate then, on all these things, and on those which are related to them, both day and night, and both alone and with like-minded companions. For if you will do this, you will never be disturbed while asleep or awake by imagined fears, but you will live like a god among men. For a man who lives among immortal blessings is in no respect like a mortal being.

One of Epicurus' students, Philodemus, beautifully sums up the Epicurean philosophy:

Men suffer the worst evils for the sake of the most alien desires. They neglect the most necessary appetites as if they were the most alien to nature. It is impossible to live pleasurably without living prudently and honorably and justly, and also without living courageously and temperately and magnanimously, and without making friends, and without being philanthropic.

Epicurus regarded himself as the originator of the true philosophy. He presented himself as a pathfinder, paving the way for his disciples and others to follow in his footsteps. He offered a plan of life that was simple and unambitious. His philosophy encourages straightforward words, good will to humankind, courtesy, loyalty to friends, gratitude for past blessings, hope for the future, and in time of trouble, patience.

CHAPTER THREE

How Epicureanism Became Established in the World Jesus Knew

Epicurus believed he had found the answer that would bring happiness to all and was anxious to spread that answer around the world. A powerful Greek ruler gave him the opportunity to do just that.

Alexander the Great was enamored of Greek culture and wanted to establish the benefits of that culture throughout the world. He built roads and established new Greek cities all the way from Egypt to Italy to Syria, making it easy for Greeks to migrate to places far beyond the boundaries of Greece itself. Epicurus took advantage of this new freedom to travel. His school was better prepared than any other Greek philosophical school to spread his message throughout the contemporary world.

Epicurus was a prolific writer, leaving behind over 300 "books" (papyrus rolls). These books were of a size and length that could be carried by anyone as they went about their daily routine. The textbooks were written for both home study and group instruction in the Epicurean schools that were being developed throughout the Hellenized world. The Epicurean missionaries carried these textbooks with them as they went out to share the message of the Epicurean way of life and were made available to anyone interested in learning about "the blessedness of a happy life." After his death, residents of the Garden organized a publishing venture, utilizing scribes to make copies of these books.

The Epicureans did not erect school buildings for the teaching of their philosophy. Their schools were established in houses, which allowed Epicureanism to spread without incurring large financial expenses. These houses served as small communes with a friendly and welcoming spirit toward strangers and potential students. No matter where they went, the cohesive bond among the Epicureans was friendship. The term they used to describe themselves was "Friends of Epicurus."

Epicureanism Spreads to Palestine

In the third century BCE Alexander the Great had imposed on all the countries he conquered, including Palestine, the Greek language, culture, and customs. Jewish merchants and businessmen learned the Greek language and customs, with many developing an interest in the philosophy of Epicurus. The Jewish youth were attracted to the athletics and pleasures of the Greek gymnasiums and became acquainted with the friendly and welcoming Epicureans and their popular philosophy of happiness. Jewish intellectuals also succumbed to the spell of this Greek philosophy.

By the middle of the second century BCE Epicureanism was so widespread in Palestine it inspired the Old Testament wisdom book of Ecclesiastes, which contains much evidence of Epicurean thought. For example, the author endorses the Epicurean wisdom that nothing is more precious to us than life itself. Ecclesiastes expressed this bit of wisdom in the following statement,

> *A living dog is better than a dead lion, for the living know that they will die but the dead do not know anything.* (Ecclesiastes 9:4)

The key development in the spread of Epicureanism into Galilee and Judea was the establishment of an Epicurean school in Antioch, in what is now modern-day Syria. In the middle of the second century BCE, the philosopher Philonides was sent to Antioch to convert the residents to Epicureanism, with the ambition of making Antioch a capital of Epicureanism. He was so highly esteemed he was invited to live in the royal court, where he made a convert of the ruler of the city, Antiochus Epiphanes, enjoying his patronage and serving for a time as an ambassador of the king.

The importance of the School in Antioch was not only its size and strength, but also its strategic location. Using the main north-south road along the Mediterranean Sea, it served as a base of operations for bringing Epicureanism into Israel.

An interesting twist of history helped pave the way for Epicureanism to become even more popular in Palestine. Near the beginning of the first century BCE, Alexander Janneus was appointed by the Greeks to be king in Palestine. He was a despotic, violent ruler who maintained his grip on the country with the aid of foreign troops. He was hated by the Jewish population. Upon his death in 78 BCE, he was succeeded by his wife, Alexandra, who proved to be a very capable ruler.

Queen Alexandra's reign was brief (78-69 BCE) but was known as a Golden Age. She introduced many social and religious reforms that were popular with the Jewish population. Most noticeably, upon the advice of her brother, a rabbi, she founded free elementary schools and made primary education compulsory for boys and girls. In the first century before Jesus, in a world full of illiteracy, among the Jews in Palestine illiteracy was all but eliminated.

Literacy among the Jews in Palestine made Epicureanism even more accessible and popular in the years leading up to the time of Jesus. In fact, Epicureanism became so popular that the Jewish religious leaders singled out Epicureanism as a special target for condemnation. The inroads made by the Epicureans on Jewish youth and culture were so threatening that their very name became legendary. They were called "Apikoros" in Greek, literally heretics. Despite the opposition of the Jewish religious establishment, Epicureanism fell on fertile soil among the businessmen, intellectuals, and common people of Palestine.

This set the stage for an inquisitive young man from the village of Nazareth to encounter this joyful Greek philosophy.

Note: In Part Five, we will carefully examine the teachings of Epicurus regarding "The Art of Well-being and Happiness"

PART TWO

DISCOVERING THE MESSAGE OF JESUS

It ain't what you know that gets you in trouble. It's what you know for sure that just ain't so.

Mark Twain, American author and humorist

Introduction to Part Two

Most people can agree on the basic historical details of the man we call Jesus: the time and place in which he lived, the fact that he inspired a large and enthusiastic following with his teaching, and the enormous influence he has had on the billions of people who have lived after him, right down to the present day. But there the agreement ends, and two major views emerge and compete.

According to one view, the view that has dominated mainstream Christianity for 2,000 years, Jesus was (and is) the one and only divine Son of God, the Savior of the world, the one who could perform miracles (walk on water, raise someone from the dead), who died to sacrificially atone for the sins of the world, was resurrected from the dead and is now dwelling in heaven with God. For mankind, entry into Heaven (salvation) and everlasting life is possible only by accepting this view. Those who do not are damned.

The other view rejects this interpretation and focuses on the actual message Jesus delivered to his followers and, ultimately, to us. It is a message of love and compassion, acceptance of every human equally, where each person is treated with dignity and respect. Whether or not Jesus is divine is open to question, but it is not the central issue. The central issue is his message, a message not of beliefs but of ethics.

It was the apostle Paul who first cast Jesus as divine and as savior of mankind. The claim that Jesus was the sole divine representative of God ultimately led to an exclusive, institutional church that has done much harm through the centuries. We now have the tools of modern scholarship to understand how and why it happened. We can also see the results of that fateful step. In Part Three of this book, we will explore this issue in further detail.

Both views can be found in the New Testament. For 2,000 years the view of Jesus as the divine Son of God has overshadowed the view of Jesus as a brilliant teacher of a way of living in this world, a way he called "the kingdom of God." But his profound teachings have largely been diminished or ignored by traditional Christianity. I invite you to join me in an historical overview of the life and teachings of Jesus of Nazareth and what happened to his teachings after he died.

CHAPTER FOUR

Jesus, The Man from Galilee

The Lost Years

It is quite surprising how little we know of most of the life of such an important person as Jesus. Except for his last three years, we have no authoritative record of his life. Only Matthew and Luke contain stories about his birth. Jesus was born into a Jewish family from the village of Nazareth, in the province of Galilee, in the nation of Israel, all occupied by Jews. Thus, Jesus was deeply immersed in the Jewish culture of that day. As a young boy he would have attended the local synagogue school, however humble it might have been. In a nation that valued education and learning, even a small village like Nazareth would have provided an educational opportunity for its children. Jesus would have learned the Hebrew scriptures, as well as the history and traditions of the nation of Israel.

Luke 2:40-52 describes an incident in Jesus' early years when he was twelve years old. His parents take him to Jerusalem to visit the holiest site of Judaism, the Temple. While there he gets separated from his parents. After a search, he is found in the Temple, astonishing the teachers with his questions and his understanding. Most biblical scholars believe this incident is a fiction composed by Luke to portray Jesus as a brilliant young person. It was common practice of biographers and historians of that period to imagine what a person would have said in certain situations and create stories to illustrate that. In any event, based on the profound wisdom of Jesus' teachings, the incident described fits our understanding of Jesus. It is easy to imagine him as an inquisitive teen-ager and young adult.

The Debate Over Who Jesus Was

His name was Jesus, which is the English version of his original Aramaic name, Jeshua, a common Hebrew name 2,000 years ago. To distinguish him from others with the same name, in his day he was probably often referred to as Jesus of Nazareth. This is the Jesus of history, sometimes referred to as the historical Jesus.

We should note the name "Jesus Christ" is a misnomer. Christ is not a name; it is a title. For 2,000 years Christians have mistakenly used the title "Christ" as if it were the last name of Jesus.

Over the centuries many titles have been given to Jesus by his followers. He has been proclaimed as the Hebrew hoped-for Messiah who would drive the hated Roman rulers out of Israel and usher in the ideal Jewish religious and political order. Jesus has been given the titles of the divine Son of God, the Savior of the World, and other such lofty titles. Through these titles we know what other people thought about Jesus. They were attempting to define who Jesus was.

The astounding fact, however, is the wide diversity of beliefs and practices these titles have produced in Christianity. There is widespread disagreement, and even conflict, about the meaning of his life and death. Numerous competing denominations, theologies, and interpretations claim to have the correct understanding of Jesus. What is often missing in these various claims regarding Jesus is a clear picture of the historical human person who created this legacy.

How did Jesus see himself? Did he believe he was the divine son of God? Did he think he was the savior of the world? Did he believe he was a divine member of the Trinity? Did he see his purpose as saving souls and getting them into heaven in the afterlife? I submit that the crucial approach is to examine Jesus' own self-image and to explore the purpose of his ministry as *he* saw it. What was he trying to accomplish?

The best way to answer the question is to pay attention to his words and his actions. We must let Jesus speak for himself. We owe him that. What he said and what he did are infinitely more important than the titles and beliefs Christians through the ages have assigned to him.

Let me acknowledge that many Christians experience Jesus Christ as a living presence in their lives. They perceive him as a real present-day companion guiding them on their spiritual journey. It is not so much the historical Jesus who lived 2,000 years ago who is important to them, but Jesus as the Christ who is a daily reality in their lives. If that is where you are in your spiritual journey, I honor and rejoice with you.

However, this presents one enormous danger. Unless our understanding of Jesus is rooted in the historical person who lived 2,000 years ago, we can easily invent a Jesus who fits our own prejudices, preferences, and politics. Instead of becoming like Jesus, it is easy to make Jesus become like us.

As Martin Luther King, Jr. noted in his piece, *The Un-Christian Christian,* religious believers "too often...have responded to Christ emotionally, but they have not responded to His teachings morally."

A clear understanding of the man from Galilee is crucial to those of us who seek to follow him. We want the Jesus whom we follow to be the same Jesus who lived and taught in Galilee almost 2,000 years ago. This means we need to pay attention to what *he* said and did.

The Four New Testament Gospels

To answer the question regarding Jesus and his purpose we begin by examining the four canonical gospels of Matthew, Mark, Luke, and John. They were written forty to seventy years after the death of Jesus and are the only biblical sources for learning what Jesus said and did.

Because the gospel writers did not know Jesus personally, they relied on stories and information about Jesus that had been passed down by word of mouth. Their goal in writing about Jesus was not to provide detailed historical accuracy, but to proclaim the "good news" (the gospel) that Jesus was the Messiah and Son of God proclaimed by Paul and the early

31

church. Thus, we would call the writers of the four gospels "evangelists" rather than "reporters" or "historians." They each wanted to express their understanding of the "good news" about Jesus of Nazareth.

Writers of history in antiquity were also storytellers. It was common practice for those who were writing about heroic figures (Alexander the Great, Julius Caesar, Augustus, etc.) to have the literary license to embellish their accounts. They were free to mix fact and fiction, attributing to a person what they felt the individual might have said or done in a certain situation.

These historical writers were not being devious. Mixing history and storytelling was the accepted practice of the day, and no one questioned whether the account was one hundred percent accurate. It was considered a true story because the author was relating what he felt to be true about the person he was describing.

The gospel writers wrote with that same freedom, each telling the story in his own way, reflecting his understanding of what Jesus said and did. As we compare the four gospels, we can discern a variety of differences in the four versions of the story. We should not let these differences disturb us. In fact, by having four different versions of the story of Jesus, we have a more complete picture of who Jesus was, and we have a better understanding of the answer to our question. It is unfair of us to demand that the gospel writers live up to our modern standards of historical writing, where we want fact and fiction to be clearly differentiated.

Two Distinctive Portraits of Jesus of Nazareth

Anyone who seeks to know who Jesus was must depend upon an examination of his words as captured in the four gospels. In so doing, a person has two choices: either to affirm all the sayings attributed to Jesus as having originated with him, or to use the best historical criteria to determine which of the sayings of Jesus probably did originate with him.

If a person chooses the first option, they are then faced with the difficulty of reconciling the version of the story found in Matthew, Mark, and Luke

32

with the version found in the gospel of John. The first three gospels are called synoptic gospels because they present a common picture of the Jesus story. When you read their accounts, they look quite similar. They present Jesus as a humble, compassionate teacher who spoke in parables and short, pithy statements. He rarely spoke about himself, and his major theme was the "kingdom of God," the way of life God wanted us to live together in this world.

The Gospel of John, however, presents a quite different account of Jesus' words and actions. In contrast to the three synoptic gospels, in John's gospel Jesus speaks in long discourses, tells no parables, and his major theme is himself and his own divinity. John presents Jesus as being co-equal with God. Instead of the humble, caring teacher of the synoptic gospels, in John's gospel there are numerous "I am" statements in which Jesus makes grandiose statements about himself (I am the Bread of Life, the Way, the Truth, and the Life, etc.).

The portrait of Jesus presented by the Gospel of John and the portrait presented by the three synoptic gospels are so different they cannot both be accurate. Since both portraits of Jesus cannot be correct, which version (John's gospel or the synoptic gospels) presents the more factual picture of Jesus?

So, what do we do? Recent discoveries and modern scholarship provide the answer.

More than ever before in history, the tools to accomplish the task of recovering the message of Jesus are available and accessible to us. Biblical scholars have developed the skills and techniques for exploring the New Testament in a more thorough manner. These developments and discoveries enable us to have a fuller understanding of the life of Jesus and his early followers.

In 1985 a major new development in biblical research was launched by New Testament scholars John Dominic Crosssan and Robert W. Funk. They gathered over one hundred biblical scholars from various universities, colleges, and seminaries to study the words attributed to

Jesus in the four New Testament gospels and other early Christian writings. They are not associated with any Christian denomination or movement. They still meet semi-annually to study, discuss, debate, and learn from one another. The advantage of their approach is that instead of the biblical scholars studying separately, the work is done collegially. Their goal has been to arrive at a consensus regarding which of the sayings and parables attributed to Jesus originated with him. They call their group The Jesus Seminar. The results of their work have been published in the book *The Five Gospels.*

The scholars of The Jesus Seminar examined over 500 sayings and parables attributed to Jesus in the New Testament, as well as other sources from the early period of the Christian movement. They identified about 100 sayings and parables attributed to Jesus as most likely to have originated with him. They have concluded the synoptic gospels of Mark, Matthew and Luke present the more historically reliable portrayal of Jesus.

These scholars view John's gospel as a meditation expressing the beliefs John, writing about seventy years after Jesus was crucified, held about Jesus and his divinity. The Gospel of John helps us understand how the writer viewed Jesus, but it is not a historically useful piece of evidence regarding the issue of who Jesus was. Yet it is primarily upon the gospel of John that Christianity bases its belief in Jesus as the Son of God and savior of the world.

A Teacher Like No Other

In the gospels of Mark, Matthew, and Luke, Jesus never claims to be divine. He does not proclaim himself as the Savior of the world, nor does he promise eternal life after death for those who believe in him. In fact, he says little about himself, and when he does, he refers to himself as a "son of man", a human being born of a human being. He uses this term eighty-seven times in the three gospels.

Based on his words in the synoptic gospels, Jesus' focus appears to be entirely on life in this world and making it better for every individual and community. These gospels emphasize Jesus' concern for others. In his actions, his sayings, and his parables, he is seen as humble and compassionate.

There is a beautiful story in Mark 10:17-18 about a man who came up to Jesus and knelt before him, asking, "Good teacher, what must I do to inherit eternal life?" Jesus responded, "Why do you call me good? No one is good but God alone."

In referring to Jesus, the gospels use a variety of titles to describe Jesus, indicating some confusion as to exactly who Jesus was. Mark, the earliest, uses sir (7:28), rabbi (9:5), son of man (9:9), teacher (9:17, 10:35 and 10:51), lord (11:3), son of David (10:47) king of the Jews (15:2), king of Israel (15:32). Another title applied to Jesus is "Master." Since this title is used to describe a master/student relationship, it reinforces the view of Jesus as a teacher. In the Gospel of Mark there are numerous references to Jesus as a Master (4:38, 9:5, 9:17, 9:38, 10:17, 20, 35; 11:21, 12:14, 19, 32). Matthew refers to Jesus as Master six times, while Luke includes many such references (3:12, 5:5, 7:40, 8:24, 45; 9:33, 38, 49; 10:25, 12:18, 18:18, 19:39, 20:21, 28, 39; 21:7).

Indeed, the title of "teacher" is mentioned more often than any other. In the Gospel of Mark alone, there are 16 references to Jesus as a teacher (1:21; 1:22, 2:13, 4:1, 4:2, 6:2, 6:6, 6:34, 8:31, 9:17, 10:1, 10:35, 10:51, 11:17, 12:35, 14:49). The other three gospels also have numerous references to Jesus as a teacher.

Jesus is also addressed as "Rabbi" throughout the gospels. In his day, the title "Rabbi" described a person who taught as an authority. It did not mean the person was a trained priest or that he had an official position in the Jewish religion but simply that the person was viewed as a wise teacher.

Thus, in the three synoptic gospels, we see Jesus portrayed predominantly as a teacher. Yet he was also a teacher like no other. He was a wisdom teacher who was also a revolutionary community organizer and ethical reformer, a teacher who cared about the well-being and happiness of each person. His message grew out of the conditions in which he lived. Israel in Jesus' day was ruled by the Roman government. The Romans controlled their vast empire by appointing client kings, as well as enlisting the aristocrats of society and the priestly elite to reign over the country and keep the rest of the population under control. Economically, Palestine was an agrarian society, characterized by a large social and economic gap between the ruling class and the peasant class. Due in part to Roman taxes and high temple tithes, for those in Galilee who owned and worked their small family farms it was a time of hardship, poverty, and cruelty.

Jesus himself came from one of the small peasant villages. He saw what was happening to the destitute peasants as they competed with one another for scarce resources, struggling to survive in any way they could. This was destroying their village life. It was in this setting that Jesus conducted his ministry.

Jesus' wise sayings and parables were designed to teach his audience a new way of being in this world. He focused on the present, not on what might happen to us after we die. He was not about what to believe, but how to live. He did not teach doctrines or theology. Rather, he taught a new and better lifestyle. This is the authentic Jesus of history.

Jesus focused on a fundamental issue and question: "We are here on this earth. How, then, shall we live?" His answer is at the heart of his message to us today, an answer that has been often ignored by traditional Christianity. It is this message that can save mankind and lead us to a life of wellbeing and happiness. It is about the art of living a life on this earth that is both happy and good. It offers guidance on how to live a fulfilling life instead of an empty one, leaving it up to individuals to make their own decisions regarding the life they choose to live.

The central theme of Jesus' message was "the kingdom of God." He used this term because most societies in antiquity were ruled by kings. It was a term people of that day would readily understand. People were looking to a king who would make things right in the world and would bring about a time of peace and fulfillment in the land.

Most of us today live as citizens of a democratic society and we no longer look for a king to bring about a peaceful and fulfilling time in our country. If, however, we ask what Jesus means by the term "kingdom of God," we discover it is his vision of life where each person is valued and is treated with respect and dignity. It is life lived on earth the way God wants it to be lived, where people have the opportunity of becoming whole persons, living in harmony with one another.

Jesus' message is profound and practical at the same time. It is also universal and is accessible to every person in every culture in every time. The lesson of how to live a good and a happy life knows no boundaries. It is for each one of us.

When we separate the teachings of the historical Jesus from the various titles ascribed to him by Paul and the early church (Savior, Lord, Son of God, Messiah), some twenty years after his death, we discover Jesus, a teacher like no other.

CHAPTER FIVE

Jesus Encounters the Epicureans

After laboring through the day under the hot Galilean sun the young construction worker began the short walk toward the "worker's camp" outside the city of Sepphoris. The new city was still under construction and was designed to be the new capital of Galilee. The young man was from the nearby village of Nazareth, only four miles away. Several months earlier he had joined the hundreds of other skilled and unskilled laborers working on the construction of this magnificent new city.

As he walked toward the worker's camp, he spotted a group of young adults sitting and chatting in front of a newly built house. He had seen them previously, and they always appeared to be a friendly and happy group of young men and women. He was curious about the group and what made them so warm and joyful. This time he decided to stop and see what this group was all about.

They welcomed him with open arms and invited him to join them for a light meal of bread and drink. He gladly accepted. As they sat around the table eating their meal, they began a gentle discussion about the philosophy of the Greek teacher, Epicurus. They treated the young man as an equal, inviting him to share his own thoughts and ideas with them. He felt right at home in their midst. This was the beginning of many happy evenings together sharing food and discussion with one another.

How was it that the young man from Nazareth and the friendly Epicureans would encounter each other in a city still under construction? Here is an answer to that question.

During Jesus' entire lifetime the ruler of Galilee was the Roman-appointed Herod Antipas, the son of the deceased Herod the Great. Antipas ruled Galilee from 4 BCE to 39 CE.

Due to an ancient dating error, the date of Jesus' birth is about 4 BCE. In the year 8 CE, when Jesus would have been about twelve years old, Herod Antipas decided to build a glorious new city that would serve as the capital of Galilee. He envisioned it as "the jewel of Galilee."

For the next fourteen years, Antipas was wholly focused on making his dream come true. He ordered that it be constructed as a Roman city with a palace, treasury, archives, forum, and public baths, along with impressive multistory buildings. It was such a beautiful new city that a few decades later the Jewish historian Josephus described the city as the "ornament of Galilee."

Antipas decided to build his new city on the site of the ruined city of Sepphoris, which had been destroyed in 4 BCE when the Roman army brutally put down an attempted Jewish revolt. For our purposes, the importance of this location is its proximity to the village of Nazareth, only four miles away, less than a two-hour walk.

For the construction of a city of this size and grandeur, hundreds, if not thousands, of laborers would be needed, both skilled and unskilled workers. The project offered the peasants of Galilee an opportunity to find long-term paid employment. Many peasants came willingly, and even eagerly, to work on this massive project. In addition, as the ruler of Galilee, Antipas had the power to conscript both skilled and unskilled workers from the peasantry to work on building the city. This adds weight to the possibility Jesus spent time working in Sepphoris.

Jesus in Sepphoris

Jesus is referred to in the gospels as a *tekton* (Mark 6:3). Many scholars accept this term to mean "skilled worker," as opposed to an unskilled day laborer. As far as we can determine, a *tekton* was engaged in various types of building repair and construction. In that role Jesus would have been a journeyman (as was his father), working on projects in Nazareth, as well as the nearby villages. However, due to the poverty in these small villages, repair and construction work would have been quite limited.

The building of Sepphoris took fourteen years. Jesus was about twelve when the construction began and about twenty-six when it ended. As Nazareth was only four miles from Sepphoris, some biblical scholars (John Dominic Crossan, Jean-Pierre Isbouts, et al.) have concluded it is quite plausible that sometime during Jesus' teen-age and young adult years, he traveled the four miles from Nazareth to Sepphoris to join the many peasants working on the massive project of building the new city. Whether he went there of his own volition, or he had been conscripted into the construction project by Antipas, is not clear.

It is not known how long Jesus may have worked in Sepphoris. Since Jesus was a skilled construction worker, he would have had a steady job working on the project and would have been paid a higher wage than he might otherwise have earned. This would have been an incentive for him to remain in Sepphoris for many if not most of those fourteen years.

I agree with those biblical scholars who have concluded it is quite plausible Jesus spent time during his later teen-age and young adult years working on the construction of Sepphoris. While we have no definitive proof Jesus worked on the building of the city, the circumstantial evidence is compelling.

Epicureans in Sepphoris

It is likely that while in Sepphoris Jesus would have encountered, and perhaps worked for, members of the Greek community there, many of whom lived by the philosophy of Epicurus. I will show that it is this philosophy which became the other major influence on the young Jesus.

Epicurus was a Greek philosopher who had a vision of extending happiness and brotherly love to all humankind. As he put it, his goal was *"to awaken the world to the blessedness of the happy life."*

40

He wrote books and trained teachers to spread his philosophy abroad. His practical philosophy appealed to the masses in every nation, and by the second century BCE, Epicureanism had reached Rome, Alexandria, and Babylon, as well as Judea and Galilee. As a result, Epicureanism became the most popular Greek philosophy in the known world for seven centuries—three before Jesus and four afterward.

The large Greek population in Sepphoris makes it quite certain that Epicureanism would have established a strong presence there and influenced the young Jesus.

The Epicureans welcomed everyone of any social class, free or slave, male or female, aristocrat or commoner, to their schools, making it easy for anyone to be comfortable there. From what we know about Jesus, this egalitarian spirit would have appealed to him. In fact, we can discern many similarities between Jesus' actions and teachings and those of the Epicureans.

Jesus after Sepphoris

It is impossible to say with certainty when Jesus left Sepphoris, or what he did when he left, for we lack any historical record on the issue. We can assume he spent several years developing his own understanding of what he wanted to do and what he wanted to say when he began his own mission to the villages of Galilee.

We do know from the gospel record that sometime between the year he would have left Sepphoris and the beginning of his mission in Galilee he joined the movement of John the Baptist in the wilderness by the Jordan river. (Mark 1:1-13; Matthew 3:1-17; Luke 3:1-22) John was an apocalyptic preacher, predicting the imminent intervention of God into history to drive out the hated Romans and restore Israel as a free and independent nation. In preparation for that coming event, he called on the Jewish people to be ready for this dramatic and decisive moment by being baptized and changing their way of life. All three of the synoptic gospels indicate Jesus was baptized by John. (Matthew 3:13ff.; Mark 1:9ff; Luke 3:21)

41

John was highly popular among the common people of Israel, and they came out to the wilderness in large numbers to hear him and be baptized by him. The Roman-appointed ruler of the northern provinces of Israel, Herod Antipas, became nervous about John's popularity and the possibility he may be stirring up the people to revolt. He had John arrested and subsequently executed.

At the time of John's arrest and execution, Jesus was still a follower of John the Baptist. At this point, he returned from the wilderness to Galilee (Mark 1:14). Jesus certainly noted that God did not come and intervene dramatically in history on behalf of Israel, as John had predicted. The next we hear of Jesus is when, at the age of thirty, Jesus begins his ministry in Galilee, with a message quite different from John's message of impending doom. (Luke 3:23)

By the time Jesus began his ministry Epicureanism was so widespread and popular in Palestine (Israel) that whether or not Jesus encountered Epicureanism at Sepphoris, it would have been almost impossible for an inquisitive young man like Jesus not to have encountered this unique Greek philosophy. It is quite likely many of Jesus' followers would also have been familiar with the teachings of Epicurus.

In addition to Epicureanism there were five other Greek philosophical schools in the time of Jesus: the Platonists, the Aristotelians, the Skeptics, the Stoics, and the Cynics. None of these schools were as popular and widespread as Epicureanism, and none was more in keeping with the teachings and lifestyle of Jesus than the friendly Epicureans.

I do not claim that Jesus was unaware of any of the other Greek philosophical schools current in and around Israel. This was a period in which there was a large amount of intellectual exchange of ideas throughout the Greco-Roman world. From everything we know of Jesus we can discern he was a perceptive and brilliant individual. The content and style of his teachings indicate his being in tune with the intellectual ferment occurring all around him. I do conclude, however, that the main connection between Jesus and the Greek philosophies was with Epicureanism.

An additional factor may have led Jesus to be drawn to the Epicurean philosophy. From his education in the Jewish synagogue in Nazareth Jesus would have been familiar with the Hebrew wisdom book of Ecclesiastes, found in the Hebrew scriptures (the Old Testament). In fact, there are significant similarities between the teachings found in Ecclesiastes and the teachings of Jesus.

Scholars have concluded the Book of Ecclesiastes was written around the year 200 BCE, about one hundred years after the time of Epicurus. There is a strong correlation between the book of Ecclesiastes and the teachings of Epicurus, indicating the author was knowledgeable about the Greek philosophy. It is possible the Book of Ecclesiastes served as a bridge for Jesus between his Jewish upbringing and his affinity for the teachings of Epicurus.

Note: For more on the relationship between Jesus and Ecclesiastes, see Appendix B.

CHAPTER SIX

Jesus' Message and Epicurus

As we explore the unique message of Jesus, it is time to examine the similarities in philosophy and teaching of two remarkable individuals who lived 300 years apart. As we shall see, there are numerous parallels between Epicurus and Jesus, both in their teachings and in their practices.

Epicurus and Jesus were both ethical teachers. Epicurus was a Greek philosophical teacher, while Jesus was a Jewish religious teacher. Epicurus was not as abstract as the Greek philosophers, nor as religious as Jesus. He captured the imagination of the public long before the time of Jesus and focused on the practical issues of human interactions. Likewise, Jesus centered his teachings on the issues of human relationships.

Epicurus and Jesus had a similar goal – to enable each human being, and humanity in general, to flourish in this life on earth. They did not speculate on abstract theological or philosophical issues. They were down-to-earth, literally, teaching humanity a new and better way to live individually and collectively with one another.

The numerous parallels between Epicurus and Jesus indicate that Jesus' teachings and practices were strongly influenced by Epicurus. I am not saying every teaching and every practice they have in common represents a direct connection from Epicurus to Jesus. There is not sufficient evidence to show that a specific instance proves a definite link between Epicurus and Jesus. However, the many correlations are too numerous to be dismissed as merely coincidental.

The Deity

Epicurus saw himself as a religious reformer, teaching humankind a more pure and positive conception of the divine. He recognized belief in the gods was common among the people of Greece and was one of the first Greek thinkers to make it his mission to help overcome the god-fearing religious traditions common at that time. He taught an understanding of the gods different from that which the masses tended to believe. He wrote:

> The impious man is not he who denies the gods of the many, but he who attaches to the gods the false opinion that most people have about them.

Epicurus taught that the gods reside in ethereal space, where they live in calm repose and continual bliss, utterly unconcerned about what happens upon this earth. They are happy, not angry, and have no interest in imposing troubles on anyone. Epicurus explained that a divine being whose happiness is perfect cannot stand in need of anything. Thus, humans cannot bestow a gift upon the gods and so win their favor nor withhold a gift and so incur their anger.

Epicurus asserted the gods are indifferent to human wickedness. The wicked are to the gods a nameless multitude, and they do not impose punishment for wickedness. The gods do not serve as enforcers of the law, which would demean their divine status, and they do not threaten humans with the prospect of punishment after death.

The one function the gods perform is to exemplify the good life of serenity, peace, and happiness. The proper attitude toward the gods is reverence because of the perfection of their bliss and the assurance this peaceful bliss will continue. The gods possess the kind of peace and happiness we humans should not only admire and revere but also seek to emulate. He believed that reverence served as a guiding force in a human life, because it was based on a correct understanding of the divine. Thus, since the gods are peaceful and have no interest in interfering in human activities, there is no reason to fear them.

Epicurus advised a friend,

> *Think of God as an imperishable and blessed creature, as the common idea of God is in outline, and attach to him nothing alien to imperishability or inappropriate to blessedness.*

Epicurus indicated that religious activities may help humans contemplate the gods and use them as examples of the serene and pleasant life. He even provides space for prayer. He believed humans have a natural inclination to pray. We should feel free to pray, he taught, because it can make us feel good and may even help guide us toward living up to our better selves. However, he did not believe the gods either hear or answer our prayers. The main value of prayer is therapeutic.

Epicurus also made this pointed comment about prayer:

> *If the gods listened to the prayers of men, all humankind would quickly perish since they constantly pray for evils to befall one another.*

The popularity of Epicurus' teaching had much to do with transforming the image of the divine from a god of wrath into a god of love. He rejected the false belief of the many that humans must fear the gods and the evils they can unleash upon humanity. He sought to allay the fear the gods will avenge themselves upon humans by causing natural disasters, or finally, the torment of hell.

In the monotheistic religion of the Hebrew scriptures (the Old Testament) the god of Judaism is often portrayed as the Greeks portrayed their gods, as an authoritative figure, a jealous, wrathful, and punishing Jehovah who is to be feared. The Hebrews' god was pictured as a lawgiver who was also a stern enforcer of that law. In Jesus' time, the newly constructed Temple in Jerusalem was populated by numerous priests and other religious officials who used the fear of God's wrath to control the population and increase their own standing and wealth within Judaism. The temple tithes and taxes they imposed became a heavy burden on the poor.

Jesus contradicted this view of God and followed the path of Epicurus, becoming the foremost proclaimer of the God of love. In fact, Jesus gave God a new name: Abba/Father. *Abba* is an Aramaic word (the language of Jesus) young children used to address their father. It is much like the English word *daddy*. It portrays God as a father, but not a stern, punishing, authoritarian Father. Rather it pictures God as a warm, loving, caring provider. This word for God, so familiar to us today, would have come as a surprising shock to his Jewish audience. It was incongruous to link the intimate word *Abba* (Daddy) with the God of the universe, but that is exactly what Jesus did. Once Jesus established the concept that God is not a punishing, angry God to be feared, but a God of compassion and love, he then focused on the issues of everyday life and how to live in this world.

Jesus proclaimed a God who values each individual life. He said:

> *Are not two sparrows sold for a penny? Yet not one of them will fall to the ground apart from your Father. And even the hairs on your head are all counted. So, do not be afraid; you are of more value than many sparrows.* (Matthew 10:29-31)

Jesus never referred to God as jealous, angry, or vengeful. He spoke only of God's love and gentle fatherhood. Like Epicurus, Jesus never talks about punishment after death. Both teachers eliminate the concept of hell, and thus the fear of hell.

Jesus did not have a whole lot to say about God. He did not have a doctrine of God. He did, however, describe the character of God:

> *Be compassionate, just as your Father is compassionate.* (Luke 6:36)

The central focus of Jesus' teaching about God was what he referred to as "the kingdom of God." This kingdom was the fulfillment of the traditional prophetic dream of an ideal society in which all distinctions of class and race have been erased. Jesus pictured and anticipated a better world to come—not in heaven, but on this earth—though it was not a religious society nor a new religion. It was simply a new lifestyle in which everyone would be treated equally.

Jesus also believed people could gain the wisdom to live in a direct relationship with God, thus eliminating the need for the temple priests. He taught that no intermediary between God and humans, including Jesus himself, was needed.

First Epicurus, and three hundred years later, Jesus, taught humanity a healthier understanding of the Deity as a God of love and compassion. There are many similarities in their teachings, which we will explore in Part Five. Here we will look at three foundational concepts they both emphasize: Nature as teacher, the simple life, and the delusion of wealth.

Three Foundations Shared in Common:

Nature as Teacher

Neither Epicurus nor Jesus appeal to a higher authority as the basis of their teaching. They appeal to nature as the common bond of every human being. Everyone depends upon nature for survival. This dependency upon nature puts everyone on equal footing. No one individual is superior to another. Nature is the great equalizer and teacher of humanity.

Epicurus taught that observing and learning from Nature is the best path to a fulfilling life. For example, he observed that every sentient being seeks to find pleasure and avoid pain. Look at the animal kingdom and you will see this principle carried out over and over. It demonstrates that seeking your own wellbeing is natural.

Epicurus also noted that following the wisdom of Nature gives one a sense of independence and learning the true values of life:

> *The one who follows nature and not idle opinion is independent in all things. As far as concerns what suffices for nature, every acquisition is wealth; but when it comes to unlimited desires, even the greatest wealth is not wealth but poverty.*

Epicurus encourages individuals to use their five senses as a guide for living. They immediately let us know what brings pleasure and what brings pain. Our five senses are better teachers than our brain. Our brain can easily fool us into believing something that causes pain is bringing us pleasure. For example, we may eat a large, sumptuous meal, thinking it is bringing us pleasure, when the result is a stomachache, heartburn, or other painful discomforts.

Epicurus adds a new dimension to Nature as a teacher:

> Gratitude is due to blessed Nature because she has made the necessities of life easy to procure and what is hard to procure unnecessary.

Seeking great wealth and the unnecessary luxuries that wealth can provide requires hard work to procure that wealth and more hard work to protect it. This leads to a fretful and worrisome life. On the other hand, if one is satisfied with the necessities of life – food and drink, clothing, shelter, and a means of transportation a contented and happy life is well within reach. This is the lesson Nature teaches.

At the heart of Epicurus' wisdom is the simple and profound idea that Nature is the great teacher. It is not religion or philosophy but Nature itself that explains life and teaches the best way to live one's life.

Connect with your environment. Notice as much as you can, using your senses to see, hear, touch, taste, and smell. Appreciate Nature, and let Nature guide you toward happiness.

As a Jewish boy attending synagogue school, Jesus would have known this quote from the wisdom tradition of Israel:

> Ask the animals and they will teach you; the birds of the air and they will tell you; ask the plants of the earth and they will teach you, and the fish of the sea will declare to you. (Job 12:7-8)

With these words, the book of Job proclaims Nature as a teacher for humans. Jesus, like Epicurus, made many references to Nature as a teacher for living a happy and fulfilling life.

> *I tell you, do not worry about your life, what you will eat, or about your body, what you will wear. For life is more than food and the body more than clothing. Consider the ravens; they neither sow nor reap, they have neither storehouses nor barn, and yet God feeds them. Of how much more value are you than the birds.* (Luke 12:22-25)

> *And can any of you by worrying add a single hour to your span of life? Consider the lilies, how they grow; they neither toil nor spin; yet I tell you, even Solomon in all his glory was not clothed like one of these. But if God so clothes the grass of the field, which is alive today and tomorrow is thrown into the oven, how much more will he clothe you – you of little faith.* (Luke 12:27-28)

Jesus suggests a way of keeping life in perspective by remembering the sparrows:

> *Are not five sparrows sold for two pennies? Yet not one of them is forgotten in God's sight. Do not be afraid; you are of more value than many sparrows.* (Luke 12:6-7)

Jesus teaches that God—as reflected in Nature--has made the necessities of life easy to obtain. Adequate food, drink, and clothing are readily available, if one learns to be happy with the simple basics of life.

According to Jesus, Nature also teaches us the character of God:

> *God makes his sun to shine on the evil and on the good and sends rain on the righteous and the unrighteous.* (Matthew 5:45)

The sun and the rain reveal to us that the Divine is not a God of judgment and wrath, but a compassionate father providing for the needs of all human beings, regardless of their behavior.

Like Epicurus, Jesus uses Nature as the great teacher for humanity to learn the basic realities of life upon this earth.

The Simple life

For Epicurus and Jesus, a second foundation of a life of happiness is the simple life. Epicurus taught that the sensible pursuit of simple pleasures is the essential ingredient of such a life:

> *Simple flavors give as much pleasure as costly fare when everything that causes pain, and every feeling of want is removed. Bread and water give the most extreme pleasure when someone in need eats of them. To accustom oneself, therefore, to simple and inexpensive habits is a great ingredient towards perfecting one's health and makes one free from hesitation in facing the necessary affairs of life.*

This means being content with little, for this is what makes freedom from worry possible. According to Epicurus, the simple life provides a sense of security; it renders the individual *"unshrinking before the inevitable vicissitudes of life"* and *"fearless in the face of Fortune."* A person who lives well within their means is not filled with anxiety and worry about the unexpected difficulties of life, which are sure to arise.

The key to the simple life is understanding the different kinds of desires humans experience. Epicurus wrote:

> *Of the desires, some are natural and necessary, some are natural but not necessary, and others are neither natural nor necessary.*

Epicurus listed the natural and necessary desires as four: food, drink, clothing, and housing.

Jesus also advocated the simple life as the fulfilling and happy way to live. He may have had Epicurus' list of the natural and necessary desires in mind when he said:

> *Therefore, I tell you, do not worry about your life, what you will eat or what you will drink, or about your body, what you will wear. Is not life more than food and the body more than clothing?* (Matthew 6:25)

We can assume Jesus followed this same simple lifestyle. He would not have been able to win over devoted followers if he instructed them to practice a simple life, while he lived a life of comfort and luxury. Of his own life of simplicity, Jesus said,

> *Foxes have holes, and birds of the air have nests, but the son of man (Jesus) has nowhere to lay his head.* (Luke 9:58)

In Luke 12:23, Jesus reminded his followers, *"Remember, there is more to living than food and clothing."*

Jesus also noted how useless it is to be anxious about life:

> *Can any of you add one hour to your life by fretting about it? If you cannot do a little thing like that, why do you worry about the rest?* (Luke 12:25-26)

Like Epicurus, Jesus taught simplicity as the way to a life of well-being and happiness, with Nature as the supreme teacher. Their teachings fly in the face of the normal way most people live in a consumption-oriented society. They are challenging the notion that the acquisition of more stuff will bring on happiness. It is a call to see life from the side of Nature, where the basic necessities of life are easy to obtain, while the luxuries of life are harder to attain and require greater and greater wealth to be able to afford them. Epicurus sums it up in this poignant statement:

> *Great abundance is heaped up as the result of brutalizing labor, but a miserable life is the result.*

The Delusion of Wealth

The correlation between Epicurus and Jesus can been seen quite clearly when we compare the topic of wealth, fame, and power. About the subject of wealth and the deceitfulness of riches each had much to teach us.

Epicurus believed the ills of human beings are caused by the delusion that greater wealth brings greater well-being and happiness:

> Neither is the turmoil of the soul dispelled nor any worthwhile happiness begotten either by possession of the greatest wealth or by honor and glamor in public life or by any other of the boundless ambitions of men.

Epicurus also made these observations about the deceitfulness of wealth:

> It is better for you to be free of fear lying upon a pallet than to have a golden couch and a rich table and be full of trouble.

> The misfortune of the wise is better than the prosperity of the fool.

The irony of life, says Epicurus, is that *"poverty, when measured by the natural purpose of life, is great wealth, but unlimited wealth is poverty."*

Jesus also spoke out strongly regarding the illusion and futility of seeking happiness through wealth. He noted:

> How hard it will be for those who have wealth to enter the kingdom of God! It is easier for a camel to go through the eye of a needle than for someone who is rich to enter the kingdom of God. (Mark 10:23, 25)

Jesus offered a vision of a way of life that stands in opposition to the normal ways the world operates. The obtaining of money and wealth may seem to be the normal way society operates. However, it is false in the sense that it is simply a way in which a society chooses to operate.

Wealth and money create a value system where the people at the top are considered important and those at the bottom are considered unimportant or even expendable. Jesus implemented a different value system that displaces the relationship to money with a relationship to human beings, where each person is valued and respected. Jesus makes it clear that "those who have wealth" will not want to enter that alternative lifestyle where sharing and caring for one another supersedes the value of money and wealth.

Like Epicurus, Jesus warned of the deceitful lure of wealth:

> *Take care! Be on your guard against all kinds of greed, for one's life does not consist in the abundance of possessions.* (Luke 12:15)

It is clear Epicurus and Jesus had the same profound understanding of the delusion of wealth. People are prone to believe a relationship to money and things brings happiness and joy. Epicurus sought to help people overcome this "false opinion," and three hundred years later Jesus joined him in this endeavor.

CHAPTER SEVEN

Similarities in Their Practices

In addition to the similarities in the teaching of Epicurus and Jesus, they had some significant practices in common. These similarities are further indications that Epicurus was a major influence on Jesus.

Egalitarianism: Everyone Is Welcome

Epicurus grew up and led his philosophical school in the highly class-conscious society of Greece. Three hundred years later Jesus conducted his ministry in the religiously class-conscious nation of Israel. Despite these prevalent, rigid class distinctions, these men were each known for their open and inclusive egalitarian spirit where each person was welcomed on an equal basis. Though they were roundly criticized by the elite of their respective societies for this behavior, they each remained firm in this practice, undaunted by the severe attacks on their character.

For his part, Epicurus made a dramatic departure from the practices of the other philosophical schools of Greece. The schools of the philosophers centered in the Forum of Athens were reserved for the educated male aristocrats of the nation. Unlike these philosophers, Epicurus taught in the garden of his home and welcomed men of ordinary education and social status, as well as women and slaves. Everyone could share in the communal meals and discussions, and each person was regarded as an equal.

This behavior was contrary to the strict class structure in place at that time in Greece. For his transgression of accepted norms, Epicurus sustained constant criticism, including being falsely accused of hosting drunken orgies in his home. Yet, over his lifetime, Epicurus never departed from his open, welcoming spirit to everyone.

This egalitarian spirit was sustained by the Epicureans over the next seven centuries, standing in contrast to the class-conscious societies wherever they established their Epicurean communities.

In contrast to the rigid class-conscious society of Israel, Jesus would have experienced or observed this warm, egalitarian spirit of the Epicureans. The religious elite of Israel, centered in the priestly class of the Jewish Temple in Jerusalem, were very protective of their superior status. Women were treated as inferior beings. The poor were disparaged and considered to be of a lower class. Neither the poor nor women had any personal or political power.

The occupying rulers of Israel, the Roman government, also operated in a highly structured manner. Backed by their powerful army, the Romans treated the Jewish population extremely harshly. The only exceptions to this harsh treatment were the Jewish Temple priests and the aristocratic political leaders, who were expected to keep the lower classes in their place and under control. Again, women and the poor were especially despised, being regarded as inferior by both the Jewish elite and the Roman rulers.

Jesus conducted his ministry among the peasants in the villages of Galilee at a time when the practices of the Roman rulers and the Jewish temple priests were making life extremely difficult for the peasants. He took his message to the poor and the marginalized, the outcasts, and the despised. He upset the social applecart by associating with those society considers unworthy. He even treated women as equals and counted women among his best friends and followers. He invited everyone to participate as equals in the communal lifestyle he was creating in the villages of Galilee: prostitutes, peddlers, tax collectors, Gentiles, Samaritans, and other questionable characters.

Three centuries before Jesus, Epicurus departed radically from the accepted norms of Grecian society by opening his home and his philosophical schools to everyone, even at the cost of vociferous criticism from the elites of Greece. Jesus took the same approach in his ministry in Galilee, to strong criticism from the powerful religious and political leaders of Israel. Despite this constant criticism, they each stood firm in the egalitarian practices of their respective movements.

Establishing Community Through Festive Meals Together

For Epicurus and Jesus communal meals were an important expression of the egalitarian spirit of their respective practices.

You will remember Epicurus conducted his teaching in the setting of his garden home on the outskirts of the city of Athens. This was in sharp contrast to the major philosophers of Greece, who taught in the rather impersonal setting of the Forum located in the center of Athens.

Epicurus made his garden home a welcoming place. Everyone was invited to come there to learn his practical philosophy of how to live a life of well-being and happiness. This included simple communal meals where food and drink would be shared with everyone. Then on special occasions and holidays festive meals would be served, again in the inclusive, egalitarian spirit where each person was welcomed equally.

As we read the Gospels, we get the distinct impression Jesus spent a large amount of time at communal meals with the villagers. He taught the villagers to regularly share together, in communal meals, whatever food they had available. Amazingly, when the villagers shared their food together this way, they found there was enough for everyone. Even the hungriest in the village had food to eat. These festive meals transformed the attitudes of the villagers toward one another from mistrust to joyous cooperation. Communal meals were a major practice in Jesus' ministry and must have made a profound impression upon the villagers.

These meals were open to all: rich or poor, sick or well, male or female, slave or free, Jew or Gentile, child or adult. It was a bold move on Jesus' part to deviate from the accepted norms of that society by inviting women, the poor, and other outcasts of society to these meals. This was a radical departure from the social customs of his day, where the upper class ate only with the upper class. Being invited to a festive dinner was a status symbol. The poor were never invited by the wealthy to a dinner. Thus, Jesus was roundly criticized by the elites of Israel for eating with the wrong people:

> When the scribes of the Pharisees saw that he was eating with sinners and tax collectors, they said to his disciples, "Why does he eat with tax collectors and sinners?" (Mark 2:16)

> And the Pharisees and the scribes were grumbling and saying, "This fellow welcomes sinners and eats with them." (Luke 15:2)

In these meals where everyone was invited, Jesus' words in the beatitudes, "How happy are you who are hungry! You will have a feast," became a reality in their midst. (Luke 6:21)

Epicurus and Jesus both made communal meals a central practice of their respective missions. These meals provided an opportunity for building a sense of equality and belonging among their students and followers. The closeness of the mealtime sharing served as an excellent setting for teaching. While eating together, real conversation and lively discussion could take place. It is easy to imagine many issues being talked about in the home of Epicurus, and three hundred years later, in the villages where Jesus taught.

Putting Community into Practice

Epicurus and Jesus each knew that happy and meaningful lives depended on more than the individual. They realized that individuals cannot be happy and productive without a happy and productive community. Thus, they each had a vision to create a new kind of society. In that sense, they were utopian thinkers. They grasped the fact that humans dream and hope for a better life in a better world.

They also understood we humans do not think only about the way we would like things to be better for ourselves. We also think in terms of our society, our nation, our world. Epicurus and Jesus each taught both an individual and collective vision of how life could be upon this earth.

Utopian dreams, however, must be connected to reality. They need to emerge from the way life is now. Their dreams, therefore, were not of some fanciful exotic paradise in some imagined future, either in this world or an afterlife.

Epicurus knew his vision for the world needed to be practical and possible, and followers were needed to first live out that dream in their relationships with one another and then to take it out into the world.

Epicurus put his utopian dream into action by recruiting disciples and followers who could put his vision into practice. He had three disciples who were especially close to him and would provide a solid foundation for creating a sense of community among Epicurus' students. He shared his vision with his followers and taught them the details of how to live out his vision.

Jesus followed this same pattern. He recruited disciples and followers who could help him put his teaching of the importance of community into action. Like Epicurus, he also had three "beloved" disciples who were key to his ministry of community-building: Peter, James, and John.

Jesus took his "community" of disciples and followers with him as he traveled to the villages throughout Galilee. He taught and demonstrated for the villagers a new sense of community in their relationships with one another, a way to share with and care for one another. Instead of competing with one another for scarce resources, Jesus taught them to cooperate with one another by sharing those resources. He helped them to develop a sense of community, restoring the traditional Hebrew practice of mutual communal care, as described in the Torah.

Jesus called this way of relating to one another "the kingdom of God." It was the central theme of his teaching. It is the way of compassion, caring, and love for one another. Following this way does not make one more religious, but it makes one more thoughtful and insightful. It is moving from blindly following the conventional ways of living—getting ahead, accumulating more material goods, chasing after increased wealth—to seeing there is a better way to live and following it.

Jesus taught the villages a better kind of community, a way of living together based on dignity and respect for each person, irrespective of race, gender, social class, age, or physical or mental condition.

Epicurus and Jesus taught and demonstrated with their disciples and followers the nature of human relationships and the kind of society and world we can be striving to build. They sought to help humanity to clearly see and understand the road that leads to a life that is both good and happy. At the root of all they taught was a remarkable wisdom about life and the importance of community.

Common Teaching Style

In their style of teaching Epicurus and Jesus also resembled each other. Their teachings were straightforward, as clear as they could make them. Their message was neither secret nor mysterious, neither private nor clandestine.

Epicurus rejected fancy rhetoric in the interest of clarity, which he regarded as the sole purpose of style. His teaching was characterized by an absolute commitment to veracity. He abhorred verbosity, as expressed in this cautionary statement:

> We must realize that the long discourse and the short discourse aim at the same objective.

Epicurus offered straightforward words, good will to humankind, courtesy, and considerateness, loyalty to friends, and kindness. This was an historical preview of the teaching style of Jesus, who followed this same style of gentle and clear instruction.

Epicurus and Jesus both used aphorisms (short, witty, memorable sayings) as a teaching tool. Here are four of Epicurus' aphorisms that can help us understand the popularity of his teachings:

Nothing is enough for a man for whom enough is too little.

Of contentment with little the greatest fruit is freedom.

To acquire great wealth and live a life of freedom is impossible.

It is better to recline upon a cheap cot in peace of mind than to have a gilded bedstead and a luxurious table and a soul in turmoil.

Compare these witty sayings with four of Jesus' aphorisms:

Do not let your left hand know what your right hand is doing.

Whoever wants to be first must be last.

It is not what goes into a person but what goes out that makes one unclean.

It is easier for a camel to go through the eye of a needle than for a rich man to enter the kingdom of God.

In addition to his memorable aphorisms, Jesus also used parables taken from the everyday life of his audience, the peasants of Galilee. They were about life situations the peasants could certainly relate to and understand. Jesus often ended a teaching moment with the words, *"You have ears to hear, use them!"* What this means is: "What I say is as clear and obvious as I can make it; all you have to do is listen."

Epicurus and Jesus shared a common goal in their style of teaching: speaking the truth in love. They used a plain and simple style to teach people how to flourish in their daily living with one another.

Spreading the Message

Epicureanism was the first and only Greek missionary philosophy. Three centuries later, Christianity became the first missionary religion in the world. I use the terms "missionary" and "mission" deliberately to include the way Epicurus and Jesus lived and taught, and the way their followers did as well. Both Epicurus and Jesus were intentional in planning their teachings and practices to be spread out into the larger world: for Epicurus it was beyond Greece; for Jesus it was beyond Galilee.

Epicurus designed his philosophy from the beginning to be accessible to the whole world. He believed he had found the one true philosophy that would lead to happiness for all humanity. Every alumnus of his school was encouraged to become an advocate for Epicureanism. The method was essentially "each one, teach one."

His self-expressed goal was *"to awaken the world to the blessedness of the happy life."* Inherent in his approach was a quiet, crusading spirit which enabled Epicureanism to spread over the contemporary world of his day. Epicurus and his followers were conscious of the mission of promoting human happiness.

Epicurus believed philosophy should be practical, useful, and accessible to any ordinary literate person. His approach was pragmatic; he was interested in helping people with the practical issues of human conduct. Therefore, he wrote and published over three hundred different textbooks that could be easily understood by the average literate person. They were also of such a size they could be easily transported by the Epicurean missionaries from one location to another for study and learning.

Epicureanism was the most popular philosophy in antiquity. Both Greeks and non-Greeks were becoming Epicureans. This friendly philosophy was able to penetrate not only large cities, but also small towns and villages, and even into rural areas where no philosophical schools existed. By the time of Jesus, Epicureanism was so well established in Israel it would have been almost impossible for Jesus and many of his followers to have avoided encountering the Epicurean philosophy and communities.

As the noted philosopher Dr. Norman DeWitt has indicated, the first missionary philosophy was a natural preparation for the first missionary religion. In the gospel record it is clear Jesus followed the pattern of Epicurus and intended his teachings and practices to be spread throughout Galilee and beyond. The first evidence of his intention to spread his message is Jesus himself. As a teacher, he could have followed the established practice of the famous rabbis and teachers of his day by setting up a headquarters in one location and inviting people to come learn from him.

Jesus, however, took a different approach. The gospels portray Jesus traveling continually from village to village throughout Galilee. He took his mission to where the people lived, where he could not only teach the villagers how to build a better community, but he could also demonstrate to them what that community would look like. (Mark 1:35-37 and 6:6; Luke 9:6)

When Jesus traveled to the villages of Galilee, he did not travel alone. He took an entourage of male and female followers with him. He demonstrated his message of voluntary communal sharing of meals and goods by bringing an egalitarian community with him.

Jesus also had a clear strategy for spreading his mission. He developed a specific plan to send his followers he had recruited and trained out to the Galilean villages he himself would not be able to visit. (Mark 6:7-13; Matthew 10:5-14; Luke 9:1-6 and 10:1-11)

The gospels also report that Jesus followed the pattern of Epicurus in sending them out in pairs, two by two (Mark 6:7 and Luke 10:1). In that day traveling alone was dangerous. When the two missionaries arrived in a village, they would come as friends of one another and become friends of the villagers. They would arrive with no money or supplies and would depend upon the traditional Mediterranean hospitality of the villagers. If they were rejected by the village elders and not allowed to share their message in the village, Jesus instructed his disciples to *"wipe the dust of the village off their feet"* and move on to another village.

Both Epicurus and Jesus gathered a community of disciples and followers to assist them in their respective missions to the world. Just as Epicurus numbered women in his circle of followers, so Jesus included women among his followers who traveled with him. (Luke 8:1-3)

Each of these visionary thinkers wanted their followers to go out into the world to share with humanity their vision of a new way of living in this world. As Epicurus expressed it, he wanted his happy philosophy to go *"dancing around the world,"* bringing the blissful life to everyone. Jesus told his disciples they were *"the light of the world"* and *"the salt of the earth,"* indicating he was entrusting to them his message and mission.

"In Remembrance of Me"

The regular communal meals Epicurus and Jesus shared with their followers were meals of simple food and drink. This epitomized their message of simple living.

An exception to this was that on the twentieth of each month Epicurus and his followers engaged in a festive evening banquet during which they refrained from the study and discussion of philosophy. Rather, they spent the day preparing a sumptuous meal. They baked bread, shared recipes, cooked meat and vegetables, and decorated Epicurus' home with seasonal fruits. The food and the wines were of the best quality.

These monthly banquets became so well known that outsiders began to refer to the Epicureans as "Twentyers." The Epicureans graciously accepted what was meant to be a derisive term and turned it into a positive, gladly adopting the designation "Twentyers" as a term of endearment and praise.

These monthly feasts were such a significant part of their self-identity, Epicurus in his will left provisions for the continuation of the meals, stating the funds were left...

for the assembly of my disciples which takes place on the twentieth of each month, having been established in recollection of myself.

Over the next seven centuries Epicureans throughout the Greco-Roman world held a banquet on the twentieth of each month, in remembrance of their founder.

In the same manner that the Epicureans held a communal banquet on the twentieth of each month "in recollection of Epicurus", so Jesus at the Last Supper—in the setting of a communal meal—took bread and broke it, and wine and shared it, inviting his disciples to eat and drink "in remembrance of me."

It is quite feasible that Jesus, as he shared the bread and wine with his disciples, had in mind the monthly banquets the Epicureans held in remembrance of their founder. First Epicurus, and then three hundred years later, Jesus, established a festive meal by which to be remembered through the years by their followers.

As Christianity developed over the years, this simple memorial act morphed into a ritual of worship that can only be performed by an ordained priest or minister. Instead of a pleasant meal celebrating Jesus' life and teachings, it became the somber Sacrament of Holy Communion to remember his death as a sacrifice to atone for the sins of humanity.

The Death of Jesus

As the gospels tell the story, shortly before his death, Jesus traveled to Jerusalem for the annual Jewish Passover festival. Some of his male and female followers traveled with him on this pilgrimage. While in Jerusalem, Jesus, like thousands of other Jewish pilgrims, went to the center of the Jewish religion, the holy Jerusalem Temple. During the annual Passover festival each Jewish pilgrim was expected to make a blood sacrifice in the temple for the forgiveness of one's sins. Booths were set up around the temple for the selling of small birds and animals to the pilgrims for the sacrificial act. Moneychangers were an essential part of this process, for the priests had a rule that Roman money could not be brought into the Temple. All purchases had to be made with Jewish currency. Jesus observed the vendors charging outrageous prices for the sacrificial offerings and the moneychangers imposing exorbitant exchange rates on the people.

The gospels (Mark 11:15-16, Matthew 21:12, and Luke 19:45) indicate Jesus responded by causing a major disturbance in the Temple. As they report the incident, Jesus drove the money changers from the Temple, as well as those who were selling the birds and animals. The entire blood sacrificial system and the corruption that went with it were against everything Jesus believed and had been teaching. He sought to rid the Temple of everything required for the bloody sacrifice.

His disruptive behavior led to his arrest. He was deemed a threat to the temple priests and to Rome and quickly executed by the Romans in the manner they used for common criminals—execution upon a cross. After less than three years of public ministry, Jesus' life was suddenly over. He was thirty-three years old.

PART THREE

THE LOSS OF EPICUREANISM AND JESUS OF NAZARETH

There is no duty we so underestimate as the duty to be happy. By being happy we sow anonymous benefits upon the world.

Robert Lewis Stevenson

Introduction to Part Three

The Road Not Taken

Two roads diverged in a yellow wood.
And sorry I could not travel both
And being one traveler, long I stood
And looked down one as far as I could
To where it bent in the undergrowth;
I shall be telling this with a sigh
Somewhere ages and ages hence:
Two roads diverged in a wood, and I -
I took the one less traveled by,
And that has made all the difference. -

Robert Frost

After Jesus died his followers were heartbroken, perplexed, confused, and uncertain about what would come next. Like the traveler in Robert Frost's poem, there were two paths open to those who followed Jesus. The path taken by the majority of early Christians became the dominant force in Christianity and has persisted through the centuries up to today. The other path became the path of the minority of Jesus' followers and has been the "one less traveled by." That fateful choice has made all the difference, shaping and defining much of the world as we know it today and creating a world far different from the world that would have been created if the other path had been chosen.

In his book *The Birth of Christianity,* the renowned New Testament scholar John Dominic Crossan has identified the two paths of early Christianity as the Life Tradition and the Death Tradition. I will use these two terms to trace the rest of the story of what happened to Christianity and the important consequences it has in today's world. However, Dr. Crossan is not responsible for the material in the following analysis of the two traditions. I also do not use the words "death" and "life" in a pejorative manner. Both traditions were valid choices for the early followers of Jesus. It is important, however, to distinguish these two traditions and the impact they have had on Christianity and the world for the past 2,000 years.

CHAPTER EIGHT

Two Paths

Through the centuries the prevailing assumption has been that the Christianity of today has existed from the earliest days after the death of Jesus. It has been thought to be the one and only Christianity, handed down by the apostles, those who had been with Jesus and had known him.

The reality is quite different. As we examine the period following the death of Jesus, we will gain a new perspective on the events of early Christianity. This will open our minds to new possibilities for the kind of Christianity we can have today.

Shortly after Jesus' death, some of his followers relocated from Galilee to Jerusalem, the capital city of Israel and the place where he was crucified. They believed Jesus would return here as the long-awaited Jewish messiah. According to the Book of Acts, they set up in Jerusalem an urban form of the communal lifestyle Jesus had established in the rural villages of Galilee (Acts 2:44 and 4:32-37). The group was led by James, the brother of Jesus, and the disciples, Peter and John.

Since they focused on the death and resurrection of Jesus, this branch of Christianity is described as the Death Tradition. They remained loyal to their Jewish roots. Daily, they visited the Jewish Temple in Jerusalem. They believed either Jesus or another messiah would soon come to Jerusalem to usher in a period of peace and prosperity for the Jewish people of Israel.

Of course, Jesus did not return, and over the centuries the Death Tradition morphed into something quite different from than what this small group of disciples had intended. It is the path that eventually developed the concepts of the original sin of every human being, the sacrificial death of Jesus as atonement for that sin, and the afterlife of every person being spent in either heaven or hell. Through the centuries that followed, the focus of the Death Tradition was always centered around the death of Jesus. This path taken by the Death Tradition has been the dominant form of Christianity for 2,000 years.

Following Jesus' death, others of his followers remained in the villages of Galilee where he had lived and taught. They focused their attention on his life and teachings. They lived as Jesus had taught them. In time, they produced two early documents about Jesus. Both are collections of the sayings of Jesus and neither document mentions the events leading up to Jesus' death nor do they mention his death by crucifixion, an empty tomb, any visits to a tomb, or any resurrection appearances. They also do not mention any anticipation of his future return.

This does not mean, of course, these other followers did not know about Jesus' death, but they showed no interest in providing a theological interpretation of that death. What was important to these Galilean followers was what Jesus taught them in his sayings and parables, as well as the example he had set in the way he lived his life. This approach is known as the Life Tradition of Christianity.

These two divergent paths of following Jesus, one focusing on his sacrificial death, the other on his life and teachings, co-existed in Israel for the next forty years. The Death Tradition remained centered in urban Jerusalem in southern Israel, while the Life Tradition stayed in rural Galilee in northern Israel. In between was the region of Samaria, and there is no evidence the two traditions interacted with each other. In the time since, the Death Tradition has dominated Christian thought and practice, with clearly observable, and often disturbing, results. As we examine those results and compare them with the expected results of following the Life Tradition, we will rediscover a better way of living in this world, the way that Jesus himself taught and lived.

CHAPTER NINE

Life Tradition

Because he had made a profound difference in their individual lives and in their communities, Jesus was regarded as a hero by those followers who remained in Galilee after his death. They had been with Jesus and knew him personally. Some had accompanied him as he traveled throughout Galilee. Jesus had taught these simple peasants how to flourish both as individuals and as a community, despite the oppressive rule of and hardships imposed by the Roman rulers and their religious and aristocratic Jewish enablers. He taught them to care for each other and work together. He showed them that the way to true happiness was to replace competition and striving for material gain with love and compassion. Jesus described doing so as living in the kingdom of God. These first followers of Jesus in Galilee did not worship him as a risen Christ, as did Paul's later congregations. They were not theologians or academics. They did not develop theories or beliefs about Jesus beyond recognizing him as an incredible wisdom teacher and visionary sage who had changed their lives in a dramatic and powerful way.

This message is the foundation of the Life Tradition of early Christianity. The Life Tradition makes no mention of Jesus as a divine being. To the villagers Jesus was a human being like everyone else. What made him different was his lifestyle and his brilliant teachings. He was a real-life hero who had transformed their lives. It is not difficult to comprehend why they would want to emulate his lifestyle and put into practice his sayings and parables.

The Jesus of the Life Tradition was an Epicurean Jesus. He was a joyous, life-affirming teacher who taught and modeled the ultimate supremacy and power of unconditional love for oneself and for all humankind. This love embraced all, regardless of social status or belief or any other measure that often divides people. Like Epicurus, he welcomed and accepted everyone. It is this universal love and acceptance that underlies the Life Tradition and separates it from the Death Tradition, offering hope for our world view now.

The Breakup of the Life Tradition

Why don't we know more about the Life Tradition? Through several historical twists and turns, some inadvertent, others intentional, the Life Tradition of early Christianity became the path less traveled. Eventually it was eliminated by those who championed the Death Tradition. Here is the story of what happened.

Beginning in 66 BCE the Romans annexed Israel into the Roman Empire. Israel was now living under the iron fist of Roman rule. The Romans imposed heavy taxes and tributes upon the people, leaving most of the population living in poverty and destitution. Before and during Jesus' lifetime the people of Israel chafed under the Roman oppression. There was a deep longing for God to anoint and empower a Messiah who could drive out the Romans, thereby enabling Israel to once again be an independent Jewish nation.

For one whole century no Messiah appeared, though many claimed to be that Jewish Messiah. In 66 CE, about 34 years after Jesus died, a group of Jewish zealots decided to take matters into their own hands. Their hope was that once they started a rebellion against their Romans rulers, God would send the Messiah to help them drive out the Romans.

In response to this rebellion, the Romans reacted swiftly and decisively, sending a massive military force into Israel to crush the uprising. The Roman army entered Israel from the north, employing the scorched earth policy as they marched through Israel, destroying everything in their path, brutally squelching the Jewish rebellion. No Messiah came to help the Jews in their battle to rid Israel of the Romans.

Among the first Israelites the Roman army encountered were the peaceful Jewish Galileans, including the Life Tradition followers of Jesus. The Romans killed thousands of Galileans and destroyed their villages. A few of Jesus' followers of the Life Tradition scattered into the desert regions east of Israel, while others made their way north to the city of Antioch in what is now Syria. We do not know what might have happened to those who scattered into the desert regions, but we do know the city of Antioch became a center of the Life Tradition of early Christianity.

The reader may remember the city of Antioch was the major center for the spread of Epicureanism into Israel and Egypt. When the members of the Life Tradition came to Antioch, they would have met the friendly and happy Epicureans. It would be easy for them to be comfortable with the teachings and practices of the Epicureans which, as we have seen, had many similarities with the teachings and practices of Jesus. Members of the Life Tradition could also be Epicureans, without needing to give up their allegiance to Jesus and his teachings, and without abandoning their own Jewish religious heritage. Likewise, it would have been easy for the Epicureans to become Life Tradition followers of Jesus.

We might also note that Paul, who had already founded many Death Tradition churches in Greece and Asia Minor, never established a church in Antioch. Prior to the Jewish revolt against the Romans, Paul had a blowup with Peter, who had come from Jerusalem to visit the Christian groups in Antioch. The showdown with Peter was a total failure for Paul, and he soon left Antioch, never to return. This gave room for the Life Tradition to flourish in Antioch, without interference from Paul's Death Tradition churches. However, because they were few in number and stayed primarily within a limited geographical area, these Life Tradition followers of Jesus and their understanding of Jesus as a wisdom teacher and real-life hero became the minor voice of Christian history for almost 300 years.

Since the churches founded by Paul were outside of Israel, they were not attacked by the Romans, and they could continue to promote Paul's version of the Death Tradition. Paul and his followers were free to become the dominant version of Christianity.

Although the Life Tradition continued to exist for the first three hundred years of Christianity, it was rapidly overshadowed by the Death Tradition. After Paul's death in the early 60s, bishops of the Death Tradition churches stepped up their opposition to the Life Tradition at every opportunity. They wrote treatises against any expression of the Life Tradition, labeling them as heresy. The word *heresy* comes from the Greek word meaning "choice." Heretics were simply those who chose to express their own ideas, rather than those imposed on them by the leaders of the Death Tradition. However, it was not until the early 300s that the Death Tradition gained the power to finally extinguish the Life Tradition. In the year 325 CE the Roman Emperor Constantine declared the Death Tradition of Christianity to be the official religion of the Empire. Soon after, the Death Tradition made it illegal to believe in or teach Jesus as a human being, with the punishment being torture and death. This ruling signaled the beginning of the extinction of the Life Tradition of Christianity.

CHAPTER TEN

Paul and the Death Tradition

Following the death of Jesus, some of his followers relocated from Galilee to the capital city of Jerusalem. Here we see the beginnings of the Death Tradition, with its focus on the death and resurrection of Jesus and the expectation he would soon return to Jerusalem as the risen Messiah. He would complete his mission of driving the Romans out of Israel and would then establish the nation as a land of peace and prosperity. The nation would be a light unto the world, an example of how God wanted people to live together in love and harmony, as Jesus had taught.

The author of the book of Acts describes the manner the Death Tradition followers lived together in Jerusalem, awaiting the return of Jesus the Messiah.

> All who believed were together and had all things in common; they would sell their possessions and goods and distribute the proceeds to all, as any had need. Day by day, as they spent much time together in the temple, they broke bread at home and ate their food with glad and generous hearts. (Acts 2:44-45)

> Now the whole group of those who believed were of one heart and soul, and no one claimed private ownership of any possessions, but everything they owned was held in common. (Acts 4:32)

> There was not a needy person among them, for as many as owned lands or houses sold them and brought the proceeds of what was sold. They laid it at the apostles' feet, and it was distributed to each as any had need. (Acts 4:34-35)

75

As we can discern from this portrayal, the original members of the Death Tradition were a devout and compassionate community, waiting in Jerusalem with anticipation for the return of the Messiah. These were followers of Jesus who had been with him in Galilee and were seeking to live the lifestyle taught them by Jesus.

However, the apostle Paul became the primary proponent of the Death Tradition, preaching and writing about that view throughout his life. Thirteen books of the New Testament are traditionally ascribed to Paul, although modern scholars have determined he wrote only seven of them: Romans, 1 Corinthians, 2 Corinthians, Galatians, Philippians, Philemon, and 1 Thessalonians.

Paul was a diaspora (living outside Israel) Jew raised in Tarsus, located in what is now Turkey. He was well educated in both Judaism and the Greek culture around him. Each of these factors influenced his viewpoint regarding Jesus and the Christian movement. He was probably in his early thirties when Jesus died. There is no evidence he ever met or knew Jesus personally.

At first Paul opposed the idea that Jesus was the long-awaited messiah, a key belief of the Death Tradition. Later, he came to believe Jesus was that messiah and he made several trips to Jerusalem, where he began to interact with the leaders of the Death Tradition. There is no evidence he ever met with the followers of the Life Tradition in Galilee.

Though Paul originally agreed with the central teaching of the Jerusalem community of the Death Tradition, he made one major change that has determined the direction of Christianity for two thousand years. He taught the idea of substitutionary atonement, the belief that salvation is made possible only through the death of Jesus. This teaching was new, as it was not held by either the Death Tradition or the Life Tradition at that time. Paul's unique new addition to the original beliefs caused a major rift between Paul and the followers of the Death Tradition.

Paul clearly believed that blood sacrifice was necessary for salvation. In I Corinthians 15:3 he states:

For I handed on to you as of first importance what I had in turn received: that Christ died for our sins in accordance with the scriptures.

When Paul refers to "the scriptures" he means the Old Testament, since the New Testament had not yet been written. Two distinct views of God are presented in the Old Testament. One view portrays God as a strict authoritarian deity of judgment and punishment, who demands a blood sacrifice for the sins of the Jewish people. The other view sees God as a compassionate deity who calls upon the people to be compassionate and caring toward one another, without demanding a blood sacrifice.

From the teachings of Jesus, it is clear he understood God to be a compassionate and caring deity who instructed the people on how to live their lives with each other. Paul, however, based his teaching on the part of the Old Testament that endorses the necessity of blood sacrifice for the forgiveness of sin.

Paul established his own ministry to spread his unique version of the Death Tradition. He believed he had as much authority as anyone else to speak as an apostle of Jesus Christ. He based his claim on a revelation he said he received directly from the risen Christ. He also claims his is the only correct understanding of the significance of the life and death of Jesus. He believed he had been called by God through a revelation to take his understanding of the gospel to the Jews and Gentiles who lived in his home area—Greece and Asia Minor.

Paul carried his message about Jesus to various cities outside of Israel. His plan was to first go to the local synagogue in each city and proclaim his message. Though he wanted Jews to become followers of Jesus, his greatest success was in winning over Gentiles who were admirers of the Jewish religion and its ethical lifestyle. These Gentiles were active participants and supporters in the Jewish synagogues and were known as God-fearers or God-worshippers or simply as sympathizers with Judaism. His success with these Gentiles infuriated the synagogue leaders, for he was stripping away from their synagogues some of their most important non-Jewish social and financial supporters.

The result was that Paul's churches consisted primarily of Gentiles who had become familiar with the teachings and traditions of Judaism. They were sympathetic to Judaism but had never become full-fledged members of the Jewish synagogues. Therefore, the men had never been circumcised.

The leaders of the Death Tradition in Jerusalem (Peter, John, and James, the brother of Jesus) had been companions of Jesus and knew that Paul's teaching of the requirement of a blood sacrifice was contrary to the teachings of Jesus. They traveled to Greece themselves or sent other leaders to oppose what Paul was teaching. Paul responded with outrage. In Galatians 1:6, he scolds the members of his congregation who are *"turning to a different gospel"* and are being confused *"by some who want to pervert the gospel of Christ."* He goes on to write, *"If an angel from heaven should proclaim to you a gospel contrary to what we proclaimed to you, let that one be accursed."*

Speaking of the leaders of the Death Tradition in Jerusalem, Paul writes that there were people who came *"from those who were supposed to be acknowledged leaders."* He then adds, *"those leaders contributed nothing to me"* (Galatians 2:6). He also sarcastically refers to them as *"super-apostles"* (II Corinthians 11:5) and goes on to describe them as *"false apostles, deceitful workers, disguising themselves as apostles of Christ."* (11:13)

Paul clearly does not want to accept the teachings of any other point of view than his own. He will not accept any authority but his own, even from those leaders of the Death Tradition in Jerusalem who had been present with and taught by Jesus himself.

Writing to one of the churches he founded, Paul confidently states:

> *Paul, an apostle, sent neither by human commission nor from human authorities, but through Jesus Christ and God the Father, who raised him from the dead...for I want you to know, brothers and sisters, that the gospel that was proclaimed by me is not of human origin, for I did not receive*

it from a human source, nor was I taught it, but I received it through a revelation of Jesus Christ. (Galatians 1:1-2, 11-12)

Paul's Version of the Last Supper

In his writings Paul characterizes Jesus' death on the cross as an atonement for the sins of humankind, in essence a blood sacrifice. He reinforces this concept in his description of the Last Supper of Jesus with his disciples, where he instituted a ritual meal by which his followers would remember him. Paul's is the first account in the New Testament of that event.

In Chapter Seven we noted that three centuries prior Epicurus had instituted a monthly ritual meal to be held by his followers *"in recollection of himself."* That ritual meal was still being observed by Epicurus' followers in the time of Jesus. Since Jesus was familiar with this practice, it should not surprise us that Jesus also instituted such a ritual meal (Mark 14:22-25; Matthew 26:26-29; Luke 22:19-20).

However, the first written account of the last supper was not penned by any of the authors of the four gospels. Twenty years before the earliest gospel, Mark, was written, Paul, in a letter to the Corinthians, wrote his version of that occasion:

> *I received from our Lord what I also handed on to you, that the Lord Jesus on the night he was betrayed took a loaf of bread, and when he had given thanks, he broke it and said, "This is my body that is for you. Do this in remembrance of me." In the same way he took the cup also, after supper, saying, "This cup is the new covenant in my blood. Do this, as often as you drink it, in remembrance of me."* (I Corinthians 11:23-25)

Neither Paul nor any of the authors of the four gospels were present with Jesus at the last meal he shared with his disciples. Notice that Paul claims his version of the event came through a revelation from "the Lord." This means he had no evidence of what happened at the meal or what Jesus said at that occasion. It also means Paul is claiming that no one else had heard about it until he wrote his version of the event.

In his version, Paul turned that meal "in remembrance of" Jesus into a support of his view of salvation through blood Paul placed the words *"This is my body that is for you"* and *"This cup is the new covenant in my blood"* on the lips of Jesus to reinforce the idea that Jesus' death was a "blood sacrifice" to atone for the sins of each human being, a view rejected by Jesus.

The idea that Jesus would ask his followers to drink his blood (even symbolically) is foreign to everything Jesus stood for. As a Jew, Jesus knew that drinking blood is strictly prohibited in the Hebrew scriptures:

> *You must not eat any blood whatever, either of bird or animal, in any of your settlements. Any one of you who eats any blood shall be cut off from your kin.* (Leviticus 7: 21)

The leaders of the Death Tradition in Jerusalem also were aware of that prohibition. Acts 15:20 states that James, the brother of Jesus, insisted that one of the restrictions placed on Gentile converts was abstaining "from blood." Jesus himself and the Jerusalem Death Tradition would have rejected Paul's description of the Last Supper as a "blood sacrifice."

We should remember it was in the setting of a meal that Jesus took bread and broke it, poured wine and shared it, inviting his disciples to eat and drink *"in remembrance of me."* It would be quite natural for Jesus to have intended the ritual of remembrance to be held in the context of a meal. Jesus and his disciples shared many meals with one another as they traveled from village to village on their mission. In addition, in the various villages where Jesus taught, he offered a communal meal where everyone, no matter their social status, was welcomed.

The regular ritual observance of the Lord's Supper in both Catholic and Protestant churches, based on Paul's unique teaching of Jesus' death as a blood sacrifice, may help us better understand why Christianity has focused on the death of Jesus though the years, rather than what he taught about the God of mercy, love, and forgiveness and how we humans should interact with one another. It is highly unlikely Jesus would have wanted his death to be remembered as a "blood sacrifice."

Paul's Big Idea

For centuries, the Jews had suffered under the control of powerful nations and empires and had longed for God to send them a messiah who would deliver them from oppression. Now it was the Roman Empire that was oppressing them. Regarding Jesus, the Jewish people could not accept that the messiah would die by crucifixion at the hands of the Romans, thus ending his life in defeat, not victory. The crucifixion was the decisive evidence Jesus was not the long-awaited, victorious messiah.

Paul, however, came up with an idea that enabled him to make the assertion that Jesus was indeed the long-awaited messiah and son of God. He outlined his idea in the opening verses of his letter to the Romans:

> *The Gospel concerning God's Son, who was descended from David according to the flesh, and was declared to be the Son of God with power according to the spirit of holiness by resurrection from the dead.* (Romans 1:1-3)

First, Paul acknowledged Jesus was a human being, born like every other human being, that is, "according to the flesh." Paul never mentions a virgin birth. No Jew would. A virgin birth would violate the profound Jewish belief in the uniqueness of God as the one and only Supreme Being. Also, Paul does not mention any miracles or extraordinary activities of Jesus. The stories of a virgin birth and the miracle stories all come later when the four gospels are written.

Second, Paul knows Jesus did not accomplish the expected purpose of a messiah. Jesus did not defeat the Romans and drive them out of Israel. In fact, he was defeated by the Romans when he was crucified as a common criminal. However, that is not the end of the story. In fact, for Paul, the real story does not begin until after Jesus dies.

In Paul's view, because Jesus was humbly faithful to God even to death upon the cross, he had *"the spirit of holiness."* Therefore, after he died, God "declared him to be the Son of God." The evidence Paul offered for

81

this claim is the resurrection of Jesus. According to Paul, God claimed the now-dead Jesus as his Son *"by the resurrection from the dead."*

Interestingly, Paul does not try to provide any evidence of the resurrection. He does not mention an empty tomb or describe any resurrection appearances by Jesus. The empty tomb stories and resurrection stories all appear later when the four gospels are written.

The closest Paul gets to any information about the risen Christ is a list of people who have had a visionary experience of Jesus (I Corinthians 15:5-8). Paul includes himself on the list, although his experience would have been at least three years after Jesus died. He provides no descriptions of any of these visionary experiences.

According to Paul, although Jesus during his lifetime did not fulfill the expectations of a messiah and son of God, it was after his death that this human being, Jesus of Nazareth, was adopted by God to be the one and only Messiah and Son of God. In Paul's view, it was through the death of Jesus and his resurrection by God, that God reconciled the world unto himself. People were made right with God, not by good deeds or acts of kindness, but through belief in Jesus as the Christ who died for one's sins.

It is clear Paul's teaching differs from Jesus' emphasis upon everyday love and compassion in this life. Jesus' message is focused on how to live a good and meaningful life on earth. Paul's message is centered in the sacrificial death of Jesus for the sins of the world, and the necessity of believing in his death and resurrection as the saving event for one's life.

Paul's claims established his version of the Death Tradition as the only true version of Christianity and the only true religion in the world. Though Paul had never met Jesus, the message he taught became the accepted version of Christianity throughout the Roman world. The Life Tradition of Galilee and the Death Tradition of Jerusalem, taught by the followers of Jesus who knew Jesus and had been with him during his ministry, were overshadowed by Paul's version of Christianity, and were eventually erased from history by his followers. Paul's teachings have dominated Christianity ever since.

CHAPTER ELEVEN

Paul and Epicureanism

The most popular Greek philosophy in the Roman Empire during Paul's lifetime was Epicureanism. Paul was a Jew by birth, educated as an Epicurean, and during his adult years became an advocate for the belief that Jesus was the Jewish Messiah and Son of God. He was born in the city of Tarsus, the gateway to Asia and an important commercial center of the Roman Empire. The city had been open to the teachings of Epicurus for three centuries prior to Paul's time and Tarsus was an important Epicurean center.

Epicureanism is mentioned in the New Testament book of Acts. Paul is in Athens where it is noted:

> *he argued in the synagogue with the Jews and the devout persons, and in the marketplace every day with those who happened to be there. Also, some Epicurean and Stoic philosophers debated with him.* (Acts 17:16-18)

In his book, *St. Paul and Epicurus* (1953), Norman Wentworth DeWitt makes the point that many of Paul's writings are a reaction to Epicurean teachings. In fact, Paul seemed to be so familiar with the Epicurean teachings that at some point in his life he must have studied the philosophy in depth.

Paul took his ministry only to the cities of Greece and Asia Minor, where he encountered a strong Epicurean presence everywhere. Paul came teaching about a god whose son had suffered and died on a cross, was resurrected from the dead, and would return soon in Paul's lifetime to redeem Jews and Gentiles who accepted Christ's resurrection and his status as the Messiah. To the Epicureans this was pure folly and was a revival of all the ancient religious superstitions.

Paul and the Epicureans were appealing to the same audience in the cities: the educated middle class. The Epicurean method was passed from friend to friend. Each disciple delighted in carrying the handbooks of Epicurus in his tote bag and passing them along to others for study.

The Epicureans had long been furnished with suitable textbooks and naturally Paul drew upon these for his material, both because they were familiar to his Greek converts and because they were familiar to himself.

Pauline Christianity, of course, was equally dependent upon the existence of a literate public. Paul did not follow the example of Jesus, who wrote nothing, shunned the cities, and conducted his entire ministry in the small rural villages of Galilee. Paul, a product of urban life and education, headed invariably for the cities, and most of his Epistles are specifically addressed to inhabitants of cities. Paul's audience was both intelligent and literate.

Paul's letters show a love-hate relationship with Epicureanism. He admired the kindly ethics of the philosophy but rejected its viewpoint regarding the gods and spirituality. He builds upon the former while vigorously condemning the latter. Paul, however, never mentions the name of Epicurus or the philosophy of Epicureanism. To do so would undermine his claim to a special revelation from Jesus Christ and would diminish the validity of his teachings. In Paul's letters, Epicurus became "he who shall not be named."

His Admiration of the Epicurean Ethic

We begin with an area of agreement between Paul and Epicurus that may come as a surprise to the reader: they both refute the concept of hell. First, Epicurus asserted the total indifference of the gods toward human wickedness. Reciprocal to this was his teaching that these same gods were not indifferent to the pious. The significance of this view is the declaration that *"the gods are friends of the wise and the wise are friends of the gods."* On the other hand, the gods simply ignore the wicked.

As a Jew, Paul agreed with the Hebrew concept, which Jesus taught, that when one dies, the whole self is dead. There is no belief that after death, one's soul goes to either heaven or hell, because the soul does not exist apart from the body. The Hebrew term *Sheoul* has often been mistranslated as "hell." It simply means, "the abode of the dead," the site where one's body was buried. The Old Testament often describes death as a deep sleep. There is nothing harmful about a deep sleep. Though Epicurus does not describe death as a "deep sleep," he does teach that nothing harmful happens when one dies. One simply ceases to exist.

Paul also seized upon the Epicurean idea that the gods are "friends of the wise" and simply ignore the wicked. Paul divides humanity into two categories: those who believe in the resurrection and imminent return of Jesus Christ, and those who don't. The believers are recognized by God, while God simply turns his back on the latter. In Romans 1:28 Paul writes, *"Since they [the unbelievers] did not see fit to acknowledge God, God gave them up to a debased mind and to things that should be not done."* They simply stop existing when they die. Consequently, there is no place of eternal torment for unbelievers. Paul taught that the only consequence of unbelief is death. In Romans 6:23 he writes, *"The wages of sin is death."* On the other hand, Paul taught that deceased believers will be raised from the dead at the second coming of Jesus Christ, which he expected to occur in his own lifetime. Jesus, Epicurus, and Paul all abolished the concept of hell.

We can also recognize Epicurean teaching in Philippians 4:11 where Paul asserts, *"I have learned in whatsoever state I am, therewith to be content."* These words sum up the personal creed of Epicurus, *"Self-sufficiency we believe to be a great good, not that we may live on little in all circumstances, but that we may be content with little when we do not have much."*

In Philippians 3:1 Paul writes: *"Rejoice in the Lord"* and in verse 4:4 he encourages his church members to *"Rejoice in the Lord always...again I say, Rejoice."* Here he agrees with Epicurus that the Greek philosopher Plato was wrong. Plato believed that a person cannot be happy all the time. Epicurus strongly disagreed with Plato and taught that continuous happiness is possible. He wrote to a youthful follower, *"It is to continuous pleasures that I invite you."* Epicurus taught that pleasure and happiness are vital aspects of life and cannot be separated from living. Paul's reason for continuous rejoicing is different: People can be continually happy in anticipation of the imminent second coming of Jesus Christ. He believed "the Lord is at hand."

Epicurus exalted the virtue of gratitude to first rank as a factor in happiness. Paul also exhorted believers to *"give thanks in all circumstances."*

Paul agreed with Epicurus regarding obedience to the laws of the land. Epicurus had written, "Let us do everything honorably according to the laws." In Romans 13:1, Paul writes, *"Let every person be subject to the governing authorities."* Epicurus also wrote, *"The laws are enacted for the sake of the wise, not that they may do wrong, but to prevent them from suffering wrong."* In Romans 13:3, Paul writes, *"For rulers are not a deterrent to good behavior but to bad."* Clearly, Paul and Epicurus agree on their views regarding the law and civil authority.

Epicurus taught his disciples absolute truthfulness in their personal relationships. Nature, he insisted, was honest herself and demanded honesty of her devotees. To be dishonest or untruthful was deemed unworthy of a student of natural phenomena. Epicurus wrote, *"As for me, I would prefer absolute honesty, as befits the study of nature, and utter oracular sayings beneficial to all men, even if not a soul shall understand me, rather than, falling in line with popular opinions, to reap lush praise that falls from the favor of the multitude."* In another saying, Epicurus writes, *"I was never ambitious to please the multitude."* Similarly, in 1 Thessalonians verse 1:5, 6, Paul writes: *we speak, not to please mortals, but to please God. We never came with words of flattery, nor did we seek praise from mortals, whether from you or others."*

Epicurus encouraged mutual instruction and admonition. He used the word "admonish" to indicate supporting each other through friendly suggestion and advice unmixed with blame, censure, or reprimand. Each Epicurean group was expected to be more or less independent and devoted to mutual instruction and tactful encouragement. This is exactly what Paul envisioned for his newly formed Christian communities. In I Thessalonians 5:11 and 14 Paul says, *"Encourage one another and build each other up. Admonish the idlers, encourage the fainthearted, help the weak, be patient with all of them."* Epicurus urges respect for others, especially for those who are more advanced in wisdom. In I Thessalonians 5:12, Paul urges the same kind of respect: *"We appeal to you to respect those who labor among you and have charge of you and admonish you; esteem them very highly in love because of their work."*

Epicureans valued faith, hope, and love above all else, with love at the very top. They stressed the importance of brotherly love, which they called friendship. Faith to them meant faith in the doctrines, faith in their leaders, and faith in their friends. Hope meant the anticipation of future pleasures and good health.

In I Corinthians 13:13 Paul closes his beautiful chapter on love by referring to these same three qualities. *"Now abide faith, hope, and love; these three, and the greatest of these is love."* Paul defined each of these qualities differently. Faith was looking back in the past and believing that Jesus Christ was resurrected from the dead. Hope meant looking toward the future and trusting that he will soon return in a second coming. However, faith and hope are both passive qualities. Each must be activated by love, which is expressed in how we live our daily lives. For the Epicureans and for Paul love is a dynamic reality; unless it manifests itself in action, if ceases to exist.

Where Paul and Epicurean Philosophy Collide

Despite agreement on the importance of certain values, there is a fundamental philosophical conflict between Paul and the Epicureans. In Philippians 3:19 Paul writes disparagingly about the Epicurean pursuit of pleasure, claiming *"their god is the belly"* and *"they glory in their destruction."* In Paul's eyes, the flaw in the teachings of Epicurus is his conclusion that pleasure is the chief goal in life. Epicurus believed that all creatures reach out for happiness—pleasure--as the greatest good and seek to avoid pain as the greatest evil. In this same verse, Paul's reference to *"minds set on earthly things"* rejects the Epicurean focus on this earth and Nature as the basis for its whole system of ethics and design for living. Paul rejects the Epicurean concept that this earthly life is all there is. His focus is on achieving eternal life in Heaven, with this earthly life as simply a prelude to that eternal Heavenly existence. The only ticket to that eternal life is to believe that Jesus is the Son of God and the Savior of the world. Without that belief, the individual ceases to exist once he dies. Paul believes that following the Epicurean way will result in the loss of eternal life.

Yet he recognizes the strong appeal of the Epicurean philosophy. In his letter to the Galatians, verses 4:3 and 8, Paul writes, *"while we were young, we were enslaved to the elemental spirits of the world...Formerly, when you did not know God, you were enslaved to beings that by nature are not gods."* Paul is referring to the teaching of Epicurus that it is Nature which is the supreme teacher – the physical world in which we all exist. He is expressing his concern that some members of his little flock in Galatia are being drawn back into Epicureanism. In verse 3 Paul uses the word "we" which may indicate that Paul himself was once an Epicurean. In verse 9 Paul asks them, *"How can you turn back again to the weak and beggarly elemental spirits? How can you want to be enslaved to them again?"* In verses 11 and 12 Paul pleads for the sympathy of the Galatians and may have been referring to his own past as an Epicurean, *"I fear I may have labored over you in vain. Friends, I beg you, become as I am, for I too, was once like yourselves."*

Epicurus' philosophy that happiness and the good life are found in pleasure was strongly opposed by Paul and the early Christian church fathers. Due to its popularity throughout the Roman Empire, Epicureanism was viewed by the Apostle Paul and the early church as the chief rival to Christianity. When Christianity gained control of the Roman Empire in the fourth century CE, the church leaders set out to destroy the Epicurean philosophy. Sadly, using the power of the Roman military, they were successful in their endeavor. They closed all the Epicurean schools and destroyed their books and Epicureanism was lost to history for the next 1,000 years.

CHAPTER TWELVE

Death Tradition in Paul's Churches

In the year 66 CE, a group of Jewish zealots in Israel, fed up with the Roman Empire's cruel and unjust rule of Israel, led a revolt against the empire. The Jewish revolt ended in total failure. In 70 CE the Roman military quashed the revolt, with tens of thousands of Jews in Israel being killed by the Romans. Many of the followers of Jesus in both the Life and Death traditions were killed. Although Paul had already died in 64 CE, the leadership of the Christian movement shifted from Israel to the churches founded by Paul in Greece and Asia Minor, which were not affected by the revolt that had taken place. The movement had its foundational roots in the Jewish nation of Israel, but now became a movement centered in the Gentile world outside of Israel.

Now it was time for the writing of the four New Testament gospels of Mark, Matthew, Luke, and John in that order.

First Came the Stories

The mythologist Joseph Campbell is perhaps best known for his book *The Hero with a Thousand Faces,* published in 1949. In this work he traces the stories of ancient heroes. Hero stories are found in numerous ancient religions and cultures. There is a certain typical hero sequence of events, which can be found in ancient stories from all over the world and from many periods of history.

Each culture has its own story about its hero/savior. These ancient stories have many features in common: a virgin birth, a humble birthplace, a dramatic rescue of the infant, the child as a wisdom teacher, the hero experiencing betrayal and painful early death, and the hero finally overcoming death. The hero is then regarded by the people as the protector and savior.

The concept of a supernatural "god-man" was the most popular and well-known story in the ancient world. The Egyptians viewed their pharaohs as divine. The Greeks had a long history of combining the human and the divine into one entity, deifying human beings. The Romans regularly deified their emperors after death.

In each of these ancient societies, priests were authorized to offer these "god-men" sacrifices and religious ceremonies were developed for people to worship these mythological divine beings.

Next Came the Four Gospels

You will remember that following the death of Jesus the Life Tradition in Galilee regarded him as a real-life hero. He was not a god-man hero, but a human being, like everyone else, who had transformed their individual lives and the communal life of their villages. To them he was a hero.

Beginning in the 70's, following the death of Paul and the scattering of the Life and Death traditions in Israel, members of Paul's churches began to compose the four New testament gospels, filling in the blanks of the Jesus story left by Paul. The authors of Mark, Matthew, Luke, and John present Jesus not simply as a real-life hero but as a superhero who could perform deeds no other human could accomplish. In their gospels, Jesus had all the attributes found in the typical hero myth described by Joseph Campbell: a virgin birth with a divine father, rescued as an infant from danger, a precocious young man, a performer of miraculous deeds, who suffered a tragic and painful early death, and, finally, as one who achieved victory over death, as shown in his resurrection.

Today we can easily distinguish between a real-life person who performs a heroic deed and a fictional superhero (Superman, Batman, Spiderman, Wonder Woman) who perform deeds that humans are incapable of accomplishing. However, the gospels were written in the style of that day—mixing fact and fiction to describe a remarkable person, turning

Jesus from a real-life hero into a superhero. The authors knew the amazing stories were mythological. They were not trying to be devious. They were simply telling the stories of Jesus in the style of that period.

Within a generation or two, however, some leaders of Paul's Death Tradition churches began to treat the stories as history. These second and third generation church leaders mistakenly took the miraculous stories about Jesus as literal, factual events. They were aware of the similarities between the miraculous stories about Jesus and the pagan "god-man" myths of antiquity. However, to elevate the Jesus stories from the pagan myths, they made the astounding claim that the devil, prior to the life of Jesus, had placed the other hero myths in the world to discredit the Christian stories about him.

Soon literal belief in the supernatural stories about Jesus came to be required for one to be considered a Christian. Other understandings of Jesus, such as the Life Tradition, were suppressed and eventually destroyed. Jesus never asked his followers to worship him or to regard him as the divine Son of God. It was Paul and the resulting Pauline version of the Death Tradition that stamped Jesus as a superhero Savior and Son of God. The institutional church grew out of this belief, with its governing hierarchy and tight control over Christian dogma. It has dominated Christianity to this day. Here is how it happened.

CHAPTER THIRTEEN

Major Changes Made in Paul's Churches

When Paul died in the mid 60s of the first century, new leaders took over his version of the Death Tradition. However, these new leaders made dramatic and fateful changes in the churches founded by Paul, with dire consequences for Christianity and the Western world.

The Churches become Patriarchal and Hierarchal

First, they abandoned the egalitarian principles of Jesus and Paul, adopting the hierarchical control structure of the Roman political and military world. The churches now had a bishop at the top, then priests and deacons, and at the bottom of the hierarchy, the laity, as described in letters they composed that are now in the New Testament. (I Timothy 3:5 and 3:12-13; Titus 1:5-9)

Also, around the year 100 CE, Clement, the Bishop of Rome, wrote to the church at Corinth that whoever refuses to "bow the neck" and obey the church hierarchy is guilty of insubordination against the divine master himself (Christ). His letter marks a dramatic moment in the history of Christianity. For the first time, we find here the argument for dividing the church between the clergy and the laity. Even within the clergy, there is a ranking of each member, whether bishop, priest, or deacon as the bishop put it, "in his own order."

To authenticate their place at the top of the hierarchy, the bishops came up with the concept of the direct succession from the original apostles of Jesus. This conferred power and authority upon a select few and established a direct chain of command for them. This maneuver firmly established their control of Christianity.

Gone was the egalitarian spirit of Jesus and Paul, replaced by the rigid hierarchy of the Death Tradition, including the requirement that to be a member of the church strict obedience to the clergy was required, especially obedience to the presiding bishop. Christianity was now under the control and power of the clergy with the additional claim it was all divinely sanctioned.

Women Are Demoted to an Inferior Class

The leaders of the Death Tradition also demoted women to second-class status. The bishops ignored the evidence in the gospels that Jesus had women followers who traveled with him and financially supported his ministry. They also ignored the fact Paul had women leaders in his churches. This downward trend of women's place in society and the church can be traced from Jesus to Paul to the Death Tradition.

In the Jewish villages of Galilee Jesus developed communities where females and males were treated equally, and everyone was welcome. The evidence is strong that Jesus had women who traveled with him and were accepted as equals in Jesus' group of followers, most prominent of whom is Mary Magdalene (Luke 8:1-3, Mark 15:40-41, Matthew 27:55-56). In his teachings, Jesus never gave any prominence of males over females. The bishops ignored the evidence in the gospels regarding the equality between males and females in Jesus' actions and teachings.

Likewise, Paul never differentiated between the importance of male and female members of his congregations. Though the Jewish, Greek, and Roman cultures of his day proclaimed and practiced male dominance over females, Paul included women in positions of leadership in his churches. In one of his letters, Paul greeted one woman, Junia, as an outstanding apostle, senior to himself in the movement (Romans 16:7). Paul also sent greetings to both male and female leaders in his churches. (Romans 16:3, 6, 7, 13, 15)

Most famously, Paul professed his egalitarian spirit in his letter to the Galatians:

> *There is no longer Jew or Greek, there is no longer slave or free, there is no longer male and female: for all of you are one in Christ Jesus.* (Galatians 3:28)

Although they were leaders in the churches Paul founded, the bishops abandoned the egalitarian approach of Jesus and Paul, adopting the lifestyle of the pagan world around them. Women were now to be treated as inferior, second-class persons. They could no longer serve in leadership positions in the church. To accomplish this innovation, they used letters they composed, but which they claimed to have been written by Paul:

> *Wives be subject to your husbands, as you are in the Lord. For the husband is the head of the wife as Christ is the head of the churches. Just as the church is subject to Christ, so also wives ought to be, in everything, to their husbands.* (Ephesians 5:22-24)

> *Wives, be subject to your husbands, as is fitting in the Lord.* (Colossians 3:18)

> *Let a woman learn in silence in full submission. I permit no woman to teach or have authority over a man; she is to keep silent.* (I Timothy 2:11-12)

Also, these leaders interjected the following into Paul's first letter to the Corinthians. Paul did not write these words:

> *As in all the churches of the saints, women should be silent in the churches. For they are not permitted to speak, but should be subordinate, as the law also says. If there is anything they desire to know, let them ask their husbands at home. For it is shameful for a woman to speak in church.* (I Corinthians 14:34-37)

Tragically, these writings of the Death Tradition of Christianity have been used to demean and intimidate women, putting them in jeopardy of mistreatment from the male population. They have also excluded females from positions of leadership in society and in the church throughout the two thousand years history of Christianity.

The Death Tradition Claims Sole Authority

Another feature of the Death Tradition was their claim to be the one and only true version of Christianity. In quelling the Jewish rebellion of 70 CE the Romans destroyed the Life Tradition in Galilee and the Death Tradition in Jerusalem, opening the path for Paul's version of the Death Tradition to take control of the Christian movement. By the end of the first century CE, the Death Tradition had become the dominant force in Christianity. This path taken by the church has made all the difference to our understanding of Jesus, to the kind of Christianity we have had through these two thousand years, and to the history of our world.

The leaders of the Death Tradition sought to discredit any other versions of the faith, labeling them as heretical. In a letter they composed and falsely attributed to the apostle Peter, they wrote:

> *There will be false teachers among you, who will secretly bring in destructive opinions. They will even deny the Master who taught them—bringing swift destruction to themselves...because of these teachers the way of truth will be maligned. In their greed they will exploit you with deceptive words...These people, however, are like irrational animals, mere creatures of instinct, born to be caught and killed. They slander what they do not understand, and when those creatures are destroyed, they will also be destroyed, suffering the penalty for doing wrong. They are blots and blemishes, reveling in their dissipation while they feast with you. They have eyes full of adultery, insatiable for sin. They have hearts trained in greed. (II Peter 2:1-3, 12-15, 17-20)*

Ignatius, Bishop of Antioch, criticized one branch of the Life Tradition for its egalitarian practice in its communities:

So today one man is bishop and tomorrow another; the person who is a deacon today, tomorrow is a reader; the one who is a priest today is a layman tomorrow; for even on the laity they impose the functions of priesthood...they all have access equally, they listen equally, they pray equally—even pagans, if any happen to come...They also share the kiss of peace with all who come.

The Church of the Death Tradition, rather than being a transformative influence in the Roman Empire, became a tightly controlled, male dominated, hierarchical organization akin to the power structure of the empire.

The Death Tradition Develops Its Doctrines

Over the next 1,000 years the tightly controlled institutional church grew even stronger. Over the years the church developed a set of definitive doctrines that solidified the church's control of the Christian movement.

During the 4th century, the Death Tradition wrestled with the basic question: Who was Jesus? The church formulated the statement that Jesus was at once wholly human and wholly God. But what did this statement mean? Was it just a matter of Jesus being more intimate with God than other human beings, or was it his being identical with God? The church pronounced the latter to be the only true way to understand Jesus and declared that any other viewpoint was heretical. This set Christianity on the road to ignoring the human Jesus while exalting him to a divine status. This led to the emphasis on worshipping him rather than following his teachings.

The Death Tradition also developed and refined one of the most powerful control mechanisms in the world: FEAR. The church used humanity's fear of death and fear of what happens after death as a means of control. The church set up a dualistic outcome for the fate of each individual—an eternal blissful life in heaven or eternal torment in hell, with no other outcome in between. The church also claimed to hold the keys to the outcome for each individual. This control mechanism proved to be highly effective over the coming centuries.

All the church had to do was convince people to fear what might happen to them after they die. The first step was to teach that God was so offended by the disobedience of Adam and Eve in the Garden of Eden that they were condemned as sinners who deserved the punishment of being forever thrown out of paradise.

The next step was to convince people that the sin of Adam and Eve had been passed down to all humans, who are forever born as depraved sinners who deserve to spend eternity in hell. Known as the doctrine of original sin, this interpretation of the story originated with Paul but was further developed in the 5th century by Augustine of Hippo.

The doctrine assumes the story of Adam and Eve is a factual event in human history. However, the story has all the characteristics of a myth, not an historical event. Like all myths, it has a meaning and a message, but it is not the doctrine of original sin. There was no literal "fall" of two human beings in a garden.

The third step of the Death Tradition was to develop the doctrine of substitutionary atonement. The heart of this doctrine is that God sent his son to die on the cross in place of all human beings, each of whom deserves to spend eternity in hell because of their depraved nature. God is angry with humanity and only a perfect sacrifice, the death of the sinless Son of God, could appease God's anger. A Christian today might put it like this, "Jesus died to save us from our sins."

We can acknowledge that Jesus died a painful early death by crucifixion. He died because of his radical teachings and lifestyle. His death was certainly tragic, but that does not mean it was a necessary sacrifice to appease an angry, vindictive God.

The fourth step was to convince people they have a soul separate from their body that will survive death. The church leaders of the Death Tradition borrowed this concept from the Greek philosopher Plato. Unlike

Plato, traditional Judaism thought of humans as simply indivisible beings, with no soul separate from the body. There is no evidence Jesus followed Plato's teaching of humans having a soul separate from the body, especially one that lives forever after death, either in heaven or hell.

The question, the leaders of the Pauline Death Tradition taught, was not whether life would continue after death, but where it would continue—in heaven or in hell. Since no one knows or can know what, if anything, awaits us after death, there is no evidence to either support or refute the church's claim. Over the ensuing centuries, however, the church used the fear of death and eternal torment in hell as a weapon to control its followers.

The Shift from Earth to Heaven

As we have seen, Jesus focused his teachings upon this life on earth, not the afterlife. The Death Tradition shifted the emphasis of Christianity from this earth to the afterlife in heaven or hell. They even encouraged a hatred of this world. In a letter they composed and falsely attributed to the disciple John, they wrote:

> Do not love the world or the things of the world. The love of the Father is not in those who love the world; for all that is of the world—the desire of the flesh, the desire of the eyes, the pride in riches—comes not from the Father but from the world. (I John 2:15-17)

In this same period, the Death Tradition mistranslated one word from Jesus, and this changed Christianity in a dramatic way. According to Mark (1:15), as Jesus began his ministry, he used the Greek verb *metanoete,* which literally means "change your point of view" or "change your way of thinking." Jesus was referring to a change from a narcissistic way of perceiving life to one of compassion and love for others. Unfortunately, the Death Tradition translated the word into Latin as "repent." This led to a moralistic interpretation of the message of Jesus based on guilt and repentance, with little change of mind or behavior, a view still predominant to this day.

Around the year 300 CE the vast Roman Empire began to crumble. The Emperor Constantine started searching for an entity that could unite the empire. Among the many diverse religions of the empire, he found the unifying force in the tightly controlled, hierarchical Christian Church. In 325 CE he declared the Death Tradition of Christianity to be the official religion of the empire. He issued imperial decrees favoring Christianity, supported the church financially, and built basilicas.

The Death Tradition took the name "Roman Catholic Church." The word "catholic" means universal, as they claimed to not only be the only true Christian church, but also the only true religion in the world. They also held the belief they had the exclusive franchise on a ticket to heaven as well as the authority to pronounce judgment on each person. The church leaders adopted the slogan, "there is no salvation outside the church." The church was viewed as the only means by which humans could be saved from the hell they deserved. This message was proclaimed so forcefully over the next 1,000 years that no one dared to die outside the orbit of the church.

Significantly, Constantine elevated the clergy to a special status. He granted them a fixed income and exempted them from military service. They were promoted to high offices in the empire, making them more powerful than local governors. The clergy were now a spiritual elite of holy men who officially were decreed to have special gifts and wisdom the laity did not possess.

After gaining imperial support, Christianity grew increasingly strong and powerful. The leaders of the church now had control of the Roman military and launched a brutal crusade to eradicate its old rivals—the popular Epicureans and the remnants of the Life Tradition. The church leaders were especially fanatical in their hatred for their chief rival, the Epicureans. They made a point of closing every Epicurean school and destroying every copy of the writings of Epicurus and his followers, including Lucretius' highly popular epic poem, *De rerum natura* (On the Nature of Things). They were so successful in their effort to wipe out Epicureanism this gentle philosophy was lost to history for the next one thousand years.

The Death Tradition now had three traits that made it dangerous to everyone else. It had the arrogance of religious certainty (we are right and good, while everyone else is wrong and bad), the authority to enforce their beliefs on everyone, and control of the political and military power of the empire. The combination of these three traits allowed the church to impose its version of Christianity on the entire population of the empire. In the rest of this chapter, I will describe the result of the unchecked power of the Death Tradition of Christianity.

The Assault on the World

In 325 CE Emperor Constantine called the bishops of the church to meet in Nicaea to hammer out a unified set of doctrines. Then in 380 CE, at the Council of Constantinople, the bishops met again to officially establish the doctrine of the Trinity, while making the beliefs of the Life Tradition illegal. At the conclusion of that council, the Roman Emperor Theodosius issued a decree that read:

> We shall believe in the single Deity of the Father, the Son, and the Holy Spirit...We command that those persons who follow this rule shall embrace the name of Catholic Christians. The rest, however, whom We adjudge demented and insane, shall sustain the infamy of heretical dogmas, their meeting places shall not receive the name of churches, and they shall be smitten first by divine vengeance and secondly by the retribution of Our own initiative, which we shall assume in accordance with the divine judgment.

Now it had become illegal to disagree with the church, and a decree in 388 CE prohibited any public discussions of religious ideas or topics. A law was passed threatening any heretic (non-believer) in the Roman Empire with death.

During this period St. Augustine (354-430), the celebrated Doctor of the Church and Bishop of Hippo, set forth the principle *Cognite intrare*, (Compel them to enter). He based this slogan on his misuse of a parable of Jesus, where in Luke 14:23 it is written "Compel them to come in!"

That concept would be used throughout the Middle Ages to justify the church's violent suppression of dissent and other beliefs. Augustine's ideas and arguments gave the leaders of the Death Tradition the justification to use force, torture, and even death to compel obedience to the church.

All forms of pagan worship were considered criminal activity prohibited by law. In 410 the emperor Honorius issued the following decree:

> *Let all who act contrary to the sacred laws know that their creeping in their heretical superstition to worship at the most remote oracle is punishable by exile and blood, should they again by tempted to assemble at such places for criminal activities.*

These decrees, and many others, gave permission to the Christians to destroy the pagan temples, statues, and shrines within the Roman Empire. In an orgy of violence, armies of the fanatical Christian movement tore down the architectural wonders of the Greek and Roman worlds. They built bonfires of books containing any other teachings or doctrines than their own. Less organized forms of religion, philosophy, and culture were no match for the ferocious Christian army of the Death Tradition.

The Catholic Church became the dominant force in the Western world for the next 1,200 years. The leaders taught that God is a powerful, punishing, vindictive deity, and this provided the rationale for the church leaders to exercise authoritarian control over everyone. They believed they had the right to judge, condemn, and even destroy those whom they determined to hold different beliefs from themselves. With this mentality, the Death Tradition systematically destroyed both the Epicurean philosophy and the Life Tradition of Christianity and paved the way for unimaginable violence against anyone marked as a nonbeliever. Through their efforts the Epicurean philosophy and the Life Tradition of Christianity were hidden from history for almost 1,500 years.

102

The complete domination by the church during Europe's Middle Ages contributed to the collapse of Western culture in the aptly named Dark Ages. In her book, *The Dark Side of Christian History,* Helen Ellerbe has explored the history of the dark shadow of Christianity and its negative effect upon the world, especially Western civilization. While acknowledging the positive impact of Christianity (hospitals, schools, etc.), we also must be honest in examining the shadow side of the church of the Death Tradition.

Obedience to the clergy (now including a pope) was demanded of all citizens. The leaders of the church ruled as an absolute monarchy, which meant everyone else must live like a serf, accepting their lowly status in society as God's plan for their life. Any attempt to improve one's lot in life was regarded as a violation of the will of God. The result was a docile and humbled population, which was exactly what the leaders of the church wanted.

Independent thinking and creativity were stifled. It was a mortal sin to think for yourself, especially if your ideas were out of line with the teachings of the church. Free thinking was not permitted, as humanity lapsed into servile obedience. The message was clear: conform to the teachings of the church or be subject to punishment through imprisonment, torture, and death.

Christianity had a devastating effect upon education and learning. The ancient academies of learning were closed. Education was limited to the clergy. Advancements in science and technology came to a screeching halt. The masses of people were kept in a state of ignorance. Worship services were held in Latin, a language the common people could neither read nor speak.

During the Dark Ages there was little or no advancement in the arts, literature, or music in the Western world. The church leaders believed these endeavors should only enhance and support the church. Therefore, these leaders kept tight control over any artistic expressions.

The church also dominated the field of medicine, preventing any real advances in the physical care of the population. The result was the spread of disease and plagues that devasted Europe for centuries.

There was little economic progress during the Dark Ages. Most people remained mired in poverty. The church, however, amassed huge wealth during this time. The church owned a large amount of land throughout Europe, and their lands were free of taxes. The church leaders developed ingenuous means of collecting wealth and confiscating land.

CHAPTER FOURTEEN

Death Tradition Embraces Violence

The Church played the pivotal role in creating and maintaining the Dark Ages in Europe. It devastated most spheres of human endeavors. However, the story gets worse. The church was also responsible for embracing violence across Europe and beyond, resulting in the deaths of millions.

The Crusades

The Crusades began around 1,100 CE. During that time social change was in the air and the church was beginning to lose some of its control over the population. In his attempt to regain the church's power and influence, Pope Urban II in 1095 called for a Crusade to march to Jerusalem to save the holy land from the Islamic "infidels." In their Sunday messages the priests proclaimed the pope in Rome as the "holy father," whose commands must be obeyed. When the pope called for a crusade against the infidels, the able-bodied men were told they must respond. In turn, the pope promised immediate entrance into heaven for any crusader who died fighting the infidels. In that world of religious fanaticism and church dominance it was exceedingly difficult for a man to resist the pope's call to join the crusaders.

More crusades followed, aimed at other supposed enemies. The crusaders, filled with a sense of righteousness, brutally attacked the church's supposed enemies—Jews, Muslims, and anyone considered to be a heretic. They fell upon their enemies with a vengeance, raping, torturing, and killing as many people as they could. The Crusades, however, failed to enhance the strength of the church; rather, the Crusades spread bitter animosity toward the church.

The Inquisitions

The Christian Inquisition was a brutal, organized effort by the Church to control people and suppress independent thinking. It was an attempt to terrorize the population into obedience to the Church. Pope Innocent III declared, "anyone who attempted to construe a personal view of God which conflicted with the Church dogma must be burned without pity."

At first the Inquisition was controlled on the local level and was only moderately violent and deadly. However, in 1231 Pope Gregory IX established the Inquisition as a separate endeavor from the local churches. This enabled the pope to hire inquisitors who were answerable only to him. The church leaders chose inquisitors based on their eagerness to arrest and torture anyone deemed to be a heretic. Jews and Muslims were especially targeted. The inquisitors served as both prosecutor and judge and were merciless toward their victims. Confessions were wrought by torture, which became a legal option for the Church in 1252 when it was sanctioned by Pope Innocent IV. Heretics by the thousands were burned at the stake, and without evidence, women were accused of being witches, and suffered torture and death. The inquisitors were free to explore the depths of torture and cruelty. The Catholic inquisition was responsible for the persecution and execution of unknown thousands for the "crime" of not believing what the church demanded of them.

Enslavement of Indigenous Populations

In the 15th century shipbuilders in Europe developed the ability to build large sailing vessels. This enabled European explorers to sail to distant lands across the globe. In the middle of the 15th century, the Catholic Church developed a new doctrine that would have devastating effects upon indigenous populations around the globe: the Doctrine of Discovery. The doctrine had its roots in papal bulls issued by Pope Nicholas V in 1452 and 1455, specifically sanctioning and promoting the conquest, colonization, and exploitation of non-Christian lands and peoples. These decrees provided legal cover for European Christian nations to pillage and destroy non-white civilizations throughout the world. The indigenous people were indiscriminately enslaved, tortured, dehumanized, and slaughtered by the tens of thousands.

The Doctrine of Discovery was expanded in 1493 by Pope Alexander VI, shortly after Columbus' first voyage. His papal decree justified the Christian explorers' claims on land they "discovered". This decree promoted Christian domination and superiority, and has been applied in Africa, Asia, North and South America, as well as New Zealand and Australia. This ideology fueled white de facto supremacy insofar as white settlers claimed they were instruments of divine destiny and possessed cultural superiority.

Following the beginning of the Protestant Reformation in 1513, Protestant denominations of the Death Tradition in Britain and the Netherlands joined the Catholic Church in promoting the Doctrine of Discovery that invalidated the rights and sovereignty and humanity of indigenous peoples around the world.

The Doctrine of Discovery used by the Death Tradition of Catholicism and Protestantism established a spiritual, political, and legal justification for colonization, seizure of land, and brutal treatment of the native populations of the world.

CHAPTER FIFTEEN

Catholic Church and Death Tradition Lose Control

For centuries, the church had violently oppressed the population and built its wealth at the expense of the masses. There was a huge economic disparity between the clergy and the laity, as well as among the ranks of the clergy. The Catholic Pope was often the wealthiest person in Europe. Conflict and corruption within the church's religious hierarchy caused dissension and division. Among the common people there was a growing, widespread resentment of the church and its authoritarian practices.

Beginning in the 12th century, various movements, including the Lollards in England and the Waldensians in Italy and France, arose across Europe in reaction to the corrupt practices within the Catholic Church. The Church responded by forcefully (and often viciously), squelching each of these alternative movements. None of the groups could gain traction against the overwhelming power of the Church.

However, three great world-changing transformations occurred, each one adding to the inevitable loss of control the Catholic Church and the Death Tradition had exercised for over 1,000 years. This was the beginning of the Modern Era. It originated in the Christian West, but its influence spread to all parts of the world.

The Renaissance

The first transformation was the Renaissance, the leading lights of which were little aware they were taking steps toward a new world. It was primarily a time of the rediscovery of classical learning and wisdom after a long period of cultural decline under the control of the Death Tradition.

Through the centuries the Church had promoted and taught a dualistic view of reality. All life is separated into two parts, and only two parts. There is good and evil – only two options. This allowed the Church to think of itself as holy and the world, including nature, as unholy. This provided the rationale for the church to exercise its authority and control over humanity.

The crack in this dualistic wall of separation between good and evil came first from within the Church in the form of Francis of Assisi (1181-1226). Born into a wealthy family, Francis abandoned material riches to adopt a simple and frugal lifestyle. He taught Christians to value the natural world, long neglected by earlier Christianity. He regarded all earthly creatures as his brothers and sisters, and even spoke of Mother Earth. Francis saw an inherent relationship between nature, humans, and God. For him, life itself (including the natural world and humanity) was sacred and was an expression of God.

Francis founded the order of the Franciscan Friars, which produced some remarkable thinkers, including Roger Bacon, the man who took the first practical steps towards empirical science. Then followed another Franciscan, William of Ockham (1285-1347), whose practical philosophy paved the way for the Renaissance, during which humanist scholars and artists affirmed the value and creative potential in the human condition.

It was in art that the spirit of the Renaissance achieved its sharpest formulation. Three towering figures stand out: Leonardo da Vinci (1452-1519), Michelangelo (1475-1564), and Raphael (1483-1520), along with Titian (1488-1576) and Correggio (1494-1534).

The effect of the Renaissance was to help humanity break free from the mental strictures imposed by Christianity, to inspire a freedom of thought and inquiry, and unleash a new confidence in the possibilities of human life on this earth. Humanity was discovering its potential freedom and its capacity for creativity.

The Protestant Reformation

In Germany, around 1440, goldsmith Johannes Gutenberg, invented the printing press, which began the Printing Revolution. His first printing was the Bible in his native German. For the first time in history, people could read the Bible themselves, without the intervention of clergy. Gutenberg's invention opened the door for the second world-changing transformation.

On October 31, 1517, Martin Luther, a dissident Catholic priest in Germany, sent a letter to his bishop, protesting the sale of indulgences (money paid to the Church to release loved ones from Purgatory into Heaven) and other practices and teachings of the Church. These soon came to be known as the Ninety-five Theses.

The Theses were printed in Latin in several locations in Germany in 1517. In January 1518 friends of Luther translated the Ninety-five Theses from Latin into German. Using the recently invented printing press, within two weeks copies of the Theses had spread throughout Germany, and within two months had spread throughout Europe in a variety of languages.

The intention of Luther and other reformers was to reconstruct the church on the foundation of the Bible, which they saw as the sole guide for understanding the will of God. However, the Reformation opened the door to much more than the Reformers had anticipated. Once the dominating structure of Catholicism fragmented, humanity gained the freedom to express individual thoughts and ideas. There was now no way to control and suppress the human mind. One result was a wide variety of expressions of Christianity within the Protestant Reformation.

Though the Catholic Church strongly opposed Luther and tried to suppress him and his Theses, he was too popular for the church to successfully silence him. By 1526 he was forming his own church in Germany. Subsequently, other Reformers arose independently of Luther, resulting in the division of Christianity into various Protestant sects and denominations. The unity of Western Christianity under the Catholic Church was shattered once and for all.

The Reformers made several significant changes in the practices of Christianity. They abandoned the idea of purgatory, emphasized the value of one's secular work, dropped the idea of clerical celibacy, and abolished monasticism, which had been considered the highest form of Christian piety.

One thing, however, did not change in the Protestant Reformation. The Death Tradition, with its emphasis on the suffering and sacrificial death of Jesus as an atonement for the sins of depraved humanity, continued to be central to Christianity. The Death Tradition also kept in place the use of fear as a means of control, seeking to persuade people to believe that upon their death they would spend eternity in either heavenly bliss or burning hell, depending on whether they believed Jesus was the unique Son of God who died for their sins.

In that sense the Protestant Reformation was a failure. To be sure, there were reforms of some aspects of Roman Catholicism much needed and long overdue. However, the Death Tradition continued in both streams of Christianity: a Roman Catholicism that tinkered around the edges with a few structural changes, yet remained a patriarchal, hierarchical expression of the Death Tradition, and a moralistic, judgmental Protestantism that splintered into many competing sects and denominations, carrying on the fundamental beliefs of the Death Tradition.

The Death Tradition of Christianity, both the Protestant and Catholic versions, brought good (hospitals, schools, charity, and other social services) to humanity. The dark side of Christianity, however, blessed the enslavement of populations and the dictatorial rule of monarchs, as well as the terrible treatment of women as lesser persons. It also brought us the witch hunts, the European wars of religion between Catholics and Protestants, the denial of science, and pedophilia by certain religious leaders.

In the modern era some denominations have increased their emphasis on the death of Jesus as a sacrifice to appease an angry God. They have also used the hope of heaven and the threat of hell as a fear tactic to win converts to their own version of the Death Tradition of Christianity. In both the Catholic and Protestant expressions of Christianity the Death Tradition has continued to this day to be widely proclaimed as the only correct version of Christianity. Even today, the Life Tradition continues to be a minor voice in today's Christianity.

The Protestant Reformation helped to rid Christianity of some of the excesses of the Roman Catholic Church. The reality is, though, it only did half the job. The rest would await the full blossoming of the Modern Era.

The Enlightenment

The Renaissance and Protestant Reformation was followed in the 1600s by the Enlightenment and the rise of reason, beginning first in England and spreading rapidly throughout Europe, eventually establishing its center in France. The key component of the Enlightenment was that human beings could now use the standard of reason to understand our world, rather than relying on religious or political doctrines and dogmas.

The Enlightenment led to the expansion of the sciences. Despite an environment of religious fanaticism and intolerance, fomented by the Church, the Scientific Revolution could not be checked. Science and reason changed humanity's view of itself and the world in several important ways. First, it changed our view of the universe. In 1543 Copernicus developed the view the earth is not the center of the universe. Through scientific observations Galileo (1564-1642) confirmed that the earth is a globe and does not lie at the center of the universe. This went against the teaching of the Church, and he was declared to be a heretic.

An additional challenge to the teachings of the church were the scientific studies of Charles Darwin (1809-1892). He introduced the concept that all species on earth have evolved over millions of years through natural selection. This discovery was strongly opposed by the church, with many arguments arising between religion and science.

The rise of the new sciences of psychology and sociology also challenged the religious understanding of human life. Both disciplines grew out of the Enlightenment. Led by Sigmund Freud (1856-1939) and Carl Jung (1875-1961), psychology studied the inner life, apart from religious teachings. In addition, sociology studied human interactions, with the understanding it is society and culture that help make us who we are and how we interact with one another, not divine decree.

The scientific revolution of the Enlightenment challenged many important religious beliefs and showed them to be false or inadequate. In the Modern Era science has expanded around the globe and is now virtually universal. Science and reason have been so fully accepted globally it may be difficult for us today to realize the dramatic transformation the Scientific Revolution has made in our understanding of humankind and the world. The highest authority was no longer the Bible, the church, or the monarchy; it now rested in reason. The Enlightenment opened the door for humans to freely explore new ideas.

The Enlightenment replaced the dualism of Church dogma with a view of the world and the universe that emphasized its essential oneness and unity. Albert Einstein put forth the Theory of Relativity, which demonstrated that everything in the universe is connected to and influenced by everything else in the universe.

The Enlightenment led to an understanding of the value of universal education that encourages the freedom of human thought, thereby expanding the liberty of each person through the democratic process, enhancing the health and welfare of humanity, and providing the opportunity for individuals and humanity in general to flourish in a manner which our ancestors could never have dreamed.

The Enlightenment is now considered to be a watershed in the history of humankind. Many scholars view the Enlightenment as the starting point of the modern world. It has also been called the beginning of "the coming of age" of humanity. No longer were humans to be regarded as children who had to be controlled by the religious and political authorities. The

Enlightenment led to a new respect for the individual person and the freedom of thought and action.

The Enlightenment meant the religious beliefs and doctrines of the church were no longer protected from challenge and questioning. Religious beliefs would no longer be the sole arbiter of morality. The new morality would be based on reason and common sense, as well as compassion for all individuals and groups. Humans are endowed with the capacity for both reason and compassion. The well-being of humanity and our earth has become the standard of morality. The social mores of society and longstanding ideas of personal and social morality are still open to question and change.

The Enlightenment was also built on the recognition that humanity could make improvements in a variety of areas: scientific, technological, intellectual, social, and moral. This does not mean progress is inevitable or universal. Some individuals can impede progress or even try to reverse it. The Enlightenment thinkers, however, believed that progress is always possible, and they worked to encourage it.

By the nineteenth century, the Death Tradition of Christianity had lost control of humankind, but both its Catholic and Protestant versions fought back against the humanism of the Enlightenment. In their effort to hang onto their authority in the face of rational thought, Catholics declared the Pope to be "infallible" and Protestants declared the Bible to be "inerrant." In doing so, the churches often put their own moral laws and beliefs above the well-being of their followers. Daniel Defoe, English writer, journalist, merchant (1659-1731), with this little poem expressed the thoughts of many in the period of the Enlightenment:

> *Of all the plagues with which mankind are curst, Ecclesiastic tyranny is the worst.*

Surprisingly, the three transformations and the Modern Era began with the discovery of a long-lost poem that opened a vision of a brave new world. Next is the story of that discovery and its promise for a better life for all.

PART FOUR

RECOVERY OF EPICUREANISM AND JESUS THE TEACHER

CHAPTER SIXTEEN

Revival of Epicureanism and Life Tradition

The Book Hunters

The men of the Renaissance eagerly sought the rebirth of the free and creative human spirit which they believed to have flowered in the ancient world and to have been lost in the Dark Ages. Known as "book hunters," some devoted their lives to the search for the classical texts of ancient Greece and Rome. One of these book hunters was Poggio Bracciolini. He was a learned man who in the 14th century had been the apostolic secretary to several popes. However, in 1415, when Pope John XXIII was deposed and imprisoned by a rival group within the Vatican, Poggio lost his honored position. Freed from these responsibilities he became one of the book hunters seeking to recover the heritage of the ancient world. Ironically, the most promising places to search for these ancient manuscripts were the monasteries of the Roman Catholic Church.

Over the previous millennium the Church had established numerous monasteries throughout Europe. The church considered monasticism to be the highest form of Christian practice. To keep the monks from being tempted by worldly pursuits, these monasteries were built in remote sites, making them difficult places to reach or exit. Though the Church had systematically sought to destroy all vestiges of the ancient pagan world, monasteries housed many manuscripts from ancient Greece and Rome. In an effort to keep the monks busy, one of their labors was to painstakingly make handwritten copies of old manuscripts, even those the Church had sought to suppress. The monks were instructed, however, to show no curiosity or interest in the content of the manuscripts, nor could they discuss the manuscripts with their fellow monks.

In the winter of 1417 Poggio traveled to a remote monastery in Germany looking for ancient manuscripts. Through the strength of his intellect and his warm personality he gained access to the private library of that monastery. There he found a stash of old manuscripts. One of these was a manuscript that had been missing for over one thousand years, Lucretius' poem, *De rerum natura – On the Nature of Things.* While most ancient manuscripts were rather mundane in nature, and thus of little interest to the book hunters, Poggio was astute enough and skilled enough to recognize the extreme importance of this epic poem, dedicated to the philosophy of Epicurus. He had found the only remaining copy of Lucretius' poem.

Through great effort, Poggio eventually obtained a copy of the poem from the monastery. He made several copies and began to share them with some of his friends and fellow book hunters. Neither he nor they could have had any idea this poem would be a major turning point in the history of the world.

It was not long before Lucretius' poem and the Epicurean philosophy began to resonate with many of the Renaissance writers, poets, and artists. The words of this visionary Epicurean poet spread throughout Europe like a breath of fresh air.

Over the next three centuries aspects of the philosophy of Epicurus influenced and impacted the writings of some of the great Renaissance and Enlightenment thinkers of Europe, such as:

- **Thomas More** (1478-1535), an English lawyer, social philosopher, author, statesman and noted Renaissance humanist. His major work, *Utopia,* is his depiction of an ideal society based mainly on the philosophy of Epicurus.

- **Giordano Bruno** (1548-1600), an Italian Dominican friar, philosopher, and poet. He became an ardent follower of the teachings of Epicurus and was burned at the stake by the Catholic Church for spreading Epicureanism in Europe.

- **Galileo** (1564-1642), an Italian astronomer, physicist, engineer, philosopher, and author. His scientific conclusions about the universe were compatible with the Epicurean poem of Lucretius.

- **Francis Bacon** (1561-1626), an English philosopher, statesman, scientist, orator, and author. He is credited with being the father of the scientific method, following the Epicurean pattern of using reason to arrive at proper conclusions.

- **Thomas Hobbes** (1588-1679), an English philosopher, who is considered one of the founders of modern political philosophy. His major work is *Leviathan,* in which he expounds on the Epicurean concept of human nature as self-interested cooperation.

- **Rene Descartes** (1596-1650), a French philosopher, mathematician, and scientist. He was a key figure in the scientific revolution.

- **Spinoza** (1632-1677), a Jewish-Dutch philosopher, often cited as "the Prince of Philosophers." He is known for his highly developed masterpiece, *Ethics,* which draws on the ethical teachings of Epicurus.

- **John Locke** (1632-1704), an English philosopher and physician, widely regarded as one of the most influential of Enlightenment thinkers and commonly known as the "Father of Liberalism." His writings influenced many of the political philosophers of Europe, and most especially, the political philosophers of the American Revolution.

- **Isaac Newton** (1642-1726), an English mathematician, astronomer, theologian, author, and physicist. He is recognized as one of the most influential scientists of all time, and a key figure in the scientific revolution.

- **Voltaire (**1694-1778), a French Enlightenment writer, historian, and philosopher, famous for his criticism of the Catholic Church, and his advocacy of freedom of religion, freedom of speech, and separation of church and state.

- **David Hume** (1711-1776), a Scottish Enlightenment philosopher, historian, economist, and essayist. He is best known for his highly influential system of philosophical empiricism, skepticism, and naturalism, all ideas related to the philosophy of Epicurus.

The Enlightenment also promoted humanitarian values and ethics. The great thinkers replaced revelation with reason as the foundation of human knowledge and society's laws. They taught the dignity of humanity, instead of the depravity of human beings. Finally, this intellectual movement called Humanism shifted attention from death and the afterlife to this world and human life on this earth. They encouraged free thinking and free will, thus enabling individuals to flourish in their daily lives. The Enlightenment improved life in Western societies. People's lives became longer, healthier, safer, freer, and happier. The great thinkers of the Enlightenment enriched the lives of the common people and the discovery of Epicurean thought was key to this improvement.

The Utopian Dream Resurfaces

As mentioned earlier, Epicurus and Jesus were both utopian visionary thinkers and planners. They each believed the world as it is now is not the only one available. They taught that the world we inhabit can be made into a better world, and they worked to make this possibility visible.

However, during the 1,000 years (400-1400) when Europe was under the control of the Death Tradition of Christianity, utopia was *otherworldly,* to be experienced only in the afterlife (and only if you obeyed the authority of the Church and accepted its beliefs). The idea that utopia could be created in *this* world, as taught by both Epicurus and Jesus, was antithetical to the teachings of the Death Tradition.

The utopian idea that this world could be made better first arose again in Thomas More's monumental work, *Utopia,* published *in 1516.* Until that time the utopian dreams of a better life in this world had been stifled by the church. Thomas More was a Christian follower of Jesus' teachings and was also familiar with Lucretius' Epicurean poem. He based his utopian concepts on the teachings of these two great visionary teachers. He began with the idea that man rather than God was responsible for what happened upon this earth. He did not believe utopia has to wait until after death. It can happen in this life here on earth.

He describes in detail an Epicurean society of happy people who want the same happiness for everyone else. More, however, is also a realist. His utopia is linked to the way people were living at that time. He was aware of the shortcomings of the society in which he lived under the chaotic rule of King Henry VIII. Yet More was a man of high ideals and believed humanity could improve its current state of being.

Francis Bacon was also an Epicurean visionary, but of a different sort. In 1626 he wrote *The New Atlantis.* It was not a utopian vision of a new society. Rather, following the wisdom of Epicurus, he introduced human reason and science, in place of divine commandment, as the foundation of arriving at decisions and conclusions. He believed the scientific method of innovation and experimentation would enable humanity to discern the "laws of nature," leading to a better life. This concept was in keeping with the teaching of Epicurus that humanity can learn from nature the secret of living well.

Thomas More epitomized the essence of the Renaissance, while Francis Bacon reflected the spirit of The Enlightenment. Following the examples of More and Bacon, as well as other early philosophers and scientists, ordinary people began to think for themselves. People started to become aware of themselves and the possibilities of a new and better future in this life. People began listening to the philosophers, scientists, and other great thinkers who were articulating utopian visions. One result was the French Revolution and the emancipation of the common people from the control of the monarchy and the Church.

The philosophical teachings of Epicurus were revived in the 17th century and helped lay the foundations for modern science and human freedom. The great philosophical thinkers of that century and the utilitarian reformers of the centuries to come found the principles of his practical philosophy to be highly relevant, even nineteen centuries after they were first taught.

The Life Tradition Is Rekindled

During the period of the Enlightenment, the spirit of the Life Tradition of Christianity was rekindled. First, many philosophers and scientists began to consider Jesus as a human being, not a divine son of God. This led to a profound shift away from the position of the Death Tradition.

Some within the religious community began to question the views of the Church. This awakening included a renewed emphasis on the humanity of Jesus and his teachings. The invention of the printing press in 1440 made it possible for more people to read the Bible for themselves. One of them was the young theologian named Michael Servetus, born in Europe in the early 1500s. As he studied the New Testament, he was surprised to find no mention of a Trinity. He wrote a book about the absence of the Trinity in the Bible. The powerful Protestant reformer John Calvin was incensed and declared Servetus a heretic and in 1553 had him tried, convicted, and burned at the stake.

Despite fervent opposition from the Death Tradition of Christianity, pockets of the Life Tradition began to spring up across Europe. Throughout the Enlightenment years, however, the Death Tradition of Catholicism and Protestantism went to great effort to stifle any expression of an alternative Christianity, sometimes violently and sometimes through fear and intimidation. It was not enough, however, to eliminate the budding of the Life Tradition in Europe.

The Enlightenment opened the door for the beginnings of the recovery of Epicureanism and the Life Tradition. This, however, is not the end of the story. It gets better.

Note: The reader can find detailed information about the Epicurean influence on these and other great thinkers in Matthew Stewart's book *Nature's God: The Heretical Origins of the American Republic* as well as Stephan Greenblatt's work *The Swerve: How the World Became Modern.*

CHAPTER SEVENTEEN

Epicureanism and Life Tradition Come to America

The developments of the Renaissance and the Enlightenment led to the 18th century American and French Revolutions and the quest for human freedom. Until the Enlightenment period -- and a long time afterward -- human freedom was regarded in the Christian world as a dangerous phenomenon, an open door to civil unrest, rebellion, and social chaos. It was firmly established that human beings were not meant to be free; rather, they were created to be subject to a higher authority: to God (the supreme ruler), and to the king and church authorities, who derived their power directly from God. Only the church authorities determined what thoughts were acceptable, and those who deviated from the dictates of the church faced severe punishment and sometimes death.

The Renaissance and Enlightenment thinkers who claimed the right to think for themselves were called freethinkers, a term of derision. They ushered in a new way of looking at the world. Along with the freedom of thought came the affirmation of basic human rights. Until that time the emphasis was almost exclusively on the duties and responsibilities owed to the higher authorities. People had never been taught to believe they had any rights of their own. This awareness of human rights led to the founding of our American democracy.

The leading lights in the founding of America as a nation were political philosophers. They were familiar with the writings of the great thinkers of The Renaissance and The Enlightenment. They were also knowledgeable of the political and philosophical writings of the Greek and Roman classics. One of those founders, Thomas Jefferson, was a Virginia planter with an intellectual and scientific bent and a devoted follower of the teachings of Epicurus and Jesus.

In his writings Jefferson indicates he first learned about Epicurus at age 24 when he was reading a book by Diogenes Laertius, a third-century biographer of Greek philosophers. Laertius concludes his work with a long and eloquent discussion of Epicurus that includes extensive quotes from the philosopher. Jefferson was also familiar with the writings of the Roman scholar Cicero and his praise of the Epicurean philosophy.

Jefferson owned at least five copies of Lucretius' poem, *The Nature of Things*. It was one of his favorite works, underlying his convictions that human reason alone is the basis of decision-making and that the world consists only of matter and space. Epicureanism also shaped his belief in the freedom of individual thought and the affirmation of basic human rights.

Jefferson believed the moral teachings of Jesus brought balance to the philosophy of Epicurus. While Epicurus focused on how to live a good and happy life as individuals, Jesus taught humanity the way to live in relationship to others. Jefferson writes:

> *Epictetus and Epicurus give laws for governing ourselves, Jesus a supplement of the duties and charities we owe to others.*

Jefferson combined the ethical teachings of Jesus (the Life Tradition) with the philosophical teaching of Epicurus. He may have been the first person in history to bring together these two outstanding wisdom teachings. He could be described as an Epicurean follower of Jesus or a Jesus follower of Epicurus. He demonstrated there is no contradiction in being a follower of both the teachings of Jesus and the philosophy of Epicurus.

An Epicurean Declaration of Independence

The finest document of the Enlightenment period, The Declaration of Independence, is a distinctly Epicurean document. It is forward-looking and utopian. The first line– *"when in the course of human events"* – signals that the document is founded on human actions and not on divine intervention. But it is in the beginning of the second paragraph where we find the very essence of the teachings of both Epicurus and Jesus:

We hold these truths to be self-evident, that all men are created equal, that they are endowed by their Creator with certain inalienable Rights, that among these are Life, Liberty, and the pursuit of Happiness.

Jesus and Epicurus each lived in highly stratified societies in which those on different levels were decidedly unequal and where that inequality was rigidly enforced. Despite this, both men taught and practiced a doctrine of inclusion, welcoming and embracing all, regardless of social status, gender, or other attributes that often divide people. Both teachers offered a pathway toward wellbeing and happiness, what Jesus referred to as "the kingdom of God." This extended to an underlying truth that all humans are innately worthy of a good life, including "the pursuit of Happiness."

Jefferson got his initial inspiration regarding 'Life, Liberty, and the pursuit of Happiness' from the English philosopher John Locke but altered it in one significant way. Locke had written that humanity has the right to "life, liberty, and the pursuit of property." As an Epicurean, Jefferson knew the "pursuit of property" did not necessarily lead to a life well-lived. He also realized that ownership of property is discriminatory and served as the basis of social divisions between landowners and those without land. The Epicurean concept of happiness is all inclusive, an inalienable right of all human beings. That right must be recognized and supported by government and its agencies. This view is the essence of Epicureanism.

Jefferson also follows Epicurus in rejecting the old idea that governments are of divine origin when he writes, ". . . *That to secure these rights, Governments are instituted among Men, deriving their just powers from the consent of the governed."* Governments are human constructions, instituted to serve the people rather than the people serving government. Thus, because the basic rights of the people arise from the natural order of things and are inalienable, government cannot take them away.

Jefferson was not alone among our founders in embracing Epicureanism. Benjamin Franklin proclaimed that good and evil are merely "empty distinctions." Like Epicurus, he sets pleasure and pain as the standards of

124

ethics and states that, *"without virtue man can have no happiness in this world."*

In 1784, Ethan Allen, known primarily as the leader of the Green Mountain Boys of Vermont, wrote an Epicurean-based treatise titled *Reason, the Only Oracle of Man.* He believed it is humans, using free will and reason, who determine the course of history, not any deity. Along the same line, Thomas Paine wrote the Epicurean-themed pamphlet *Common Sense,* followed quickly by his monumental book, *The Age of Reason.* John Adams, James Madison, and to a lesser extent, George Washington, were also aware of and influenced by Lucretius' poem and the Epicurean philosophy.

Deism

In the 17th and 18th centuries the traditional concept of God, known as Theism, was challenged. The old view saw God as Supreme Being who possesses the qualities of omnipotence and omniscience. This all-powerful and all-knowing deity can intervene in the world and from time to time chooses to do so. Christian Theism also taught that those who believe in Jesus as the divine Son of God could ask God to act on one's behalf.

During the Enlightenment period a new understanding of God more compatible with modern science emerged. It is an Enlightenment idea and is known as Deism. Prominent European philosophers who were Deists include Thomas Hobbes, Spinoza, Thomas Locke, David Hume, Voltaire, and Rousseau. The foundation of Deism is the concept that a Supreme Being created the universe, set it in motion to operate through the Natural Laws (e.g., gravity), and then retired from the scene. God stepped out of the way and does not intervene in human affairs and does not control the events of Nature. Deism views Jesus not as the divine Son of God but as a human being who understood human nature and taught a better way of living.

Though the term Deism did not exist during the time of Epicurus, it is clear from his teachings he would find Deism compatible with his own philosophy. In his teachings, the gods exist in a blissful ethereal world and take no interest in the affairs of humans on earth and have no desire to intervene in our worldly existence.

The founders of America were familiar with Deism, and many declared themselves to be Deists. The list includes Thomas Jefferson, James Madison, Alexander Hamilton, Ethan Allen, Benjamin Franklin, George Washington, and Thomas Paine. The inclusion in the Declaration of Independence of the phrase "the Laws of Nature and Nature's God" reflects the deist viewpoint, enunciated first by Epicurus, that the deity was the creator of the natural universe, yet shows no interest in exerting power and control, or even being involved, in the activities of humans upon this earth. Whatever deity exists, they taught, is Nature's God, and is humanity's god only to the extent that humans are a part of Nature.

The moral code for Deists is based on observation of the way in which they perceive the operation of God in the universe. Thomas Paine penned these words as the foundation of the ethics of Deism:

> The only idea we can have of serving God is that of contributing to the happiness of the living creation that God has made...The moral duty of man consists in imitating the moral goodness and beneficence of God manifested in the creation toward all his creatures.

By observing nature the Deists perceived God as a benign deity as opposed to the concept of the Death Tradition of a vindictive, judgmental God. Like Epicurus, the Deists saw that Nature (God) provided the necessities of life for all creatures of the earth.

"We the People"

The founders shared Jefferson's conviction that a nation should be governed not by commandments from any supernatural being but by respect for the laws of Nature and science as revealed by reason and common sense. The Preamble to the Constitution of the United States also reflects the Epicurean viewpoint. The opening words of the Preamble declares it is "We the people of the United States" not any deity or religion who are forming "a more perfect union." The framers of the Constitution enshrined the fundamental concept that "We the people" are to be the supreme governmental authority.

The United States of America became the first nation with a "godless" constitution, in which God is deliberately not mentioned at all. This bold step broke with all cultural and historical precedents. The American Constitution is the official founding document of the world's first secular government. It makes no mention of Jesus or Christianity. The only reference to religion in the Constitution is one that restricted religion. Article 6 declares "no religious test shall ever be required as a qualification to any office or public trust under the United States."

The framers of our Constitution were aware of Europe's history of religious tyranny and violence. They did not want America to replicate the religious wars of the European past. Thomas Jefferson wrote,

> *Millions of innocent men, women, and children, since the introduction of Christianity, have been burnt, tortured, fined, and imprisoned.*

The founders did not seek to make America a godless nation, only its constitution and government. They inserted in the First Amendment the "freedom of religion" clause and prohibited the government from establishing any certain religion within the new country.

The founders of America also placed elements of the Epicurean philosophy into the Constitution In a very real sense, the founders designed America to be a secular Epicurean-style nation "of the people, by the people, and for the people," as Abraham Lincoln so eloquently expressed this ideal.

The philosophy of Epicureanism and the Life Tradition of Christianity, both focused on actions not beliefs, were now woven by the founders into the national fabric of the United States.

CHAPTER EIGHTEEN

Discovery of the Origins of the Life Tradition

From 325 CE, when the Death Tradition began destroying its churches, schools, and documents, the existence of the Life Tradition of early Christianity remained hidden from view for 1,500 years. Only in the last 150 years has the presence of the Life Tradition in early Christianity come to light. The story of the rediscovery of the Life Tradition is a fascinating saga. It began in Germany with the discovery of a book.

The Jesus Instruction Book (The Sayings Gospel Q)

Within the first ten or fifteen years after the death of Jesus, in the widespread ancient practice of wisdom schools, the Galilean followers of Jesus collected his sayings and parables into a book. As the Death Tradition sought to eliminate all vestiges of the Life Tradition, it confiscated and burned all copies of this premier book. However, unlike many other ancient manuscripts, this book was not found in an archeological dig or in a monastery. It was not until the middle of the 19th century that German scholars identified this collection of the sayings of Jesus. Remarkably, all these years it has been embedded in the New Testament gospels of Matthew and Luke.

Here is how they made the discovery. The scholars realized Mark was the first gospel to be written, sometime between 70-75 CE, about forty years after Jesus died. Fifteen years or so later, Luke and Matthew independently wrote their gospels. They each used Mark as the basic source of their gospels, editing and expanding Mark to suit their individual purposes.

Around the 1840s the German biblical scholars noticed that Matthew and Luke have about 250 verses in common not found anywhere in Mark. Since Matthew and Luke wrote independently of each other, the question naturally arose: How did they come by this shared material not originating in Mark? The scholars concluded that Matthew and Luke used an additional written source in the composition of their respective gospels, a source not known to Mark, or at least not used by Mark. By examining the verses Matthew and Luke had in common, but not found in Mark, they were able to reconstruct this previously unknown document.

It turns out this document is a collection of the sayings of Jesus. We are fortunate that Matthew and Luke each had a copy of the document, and each decided to include material from the document in their gospel. Since this document was the source of many of the teachings of Jesus, the scholars gave it the name Quelle, the German word for "source." Over the years it has become known as The Sayings Gospel Q. It can be read as a Jesus Instruction Book. It was evidently used by the Life Tradition of his Galilean followers in their house churches and/or schools.

The fact that several Galilean cities are named in the document, often in a negative light (Luke 19:13-15), indicates the sayings collection originated in Galilee, the center of the Life Tradition of early Christianity.

The book contains no information about Jesus' birth, life, or death. There are no miracle stories and no mention of a resurrection or any resurrection appearances. It does not ascribe to Jesus any exalted titles, such as "Son of God," "Messiah," or "Savior." It never uses the word "Christ."

In this document there is no call to "believe in Jesus" as a divine being. There is no indication Jesus believed he was divine, or that his mission was to "save souls," or that his death would bring salvation to individuals and provide entrance into heaven.

The Sayings Gospel Q is written in the style and pattern of the wisdom teachings of both Epicurus and the Jewish wisdom tradition. This document connects us to those two wisdom traditions and reinforces the concept that Jesus taught in the style of both wisdom traditions.

Why are there no known original copies of the sayings Gospel Q available today? We know Matthew and Luke each had a copy. We would assume a collection of the sayings of Jesus would be highly valued and certainly preserved. What happened to their two copies, as well as other copies of the document? In their mission to destroy all materials of the Life Tradition, apparently the leaders of the Death Tradition were successful, for until this day we have no actual copies of The Sayings Gospel Q.

Thanks to the work of the German biblical scholars, we now know there was an ancient document containing the sayings of Jesus, used by his Galilean followers of the Life Tradition, which Luke and Matthew included in their gospels. This was the first step in the rediscovery of the Life Tradition of early Christianity.

A Second Document of the Life Tradition

The Life Tradition of early Christianity also produced a second collection of the Sayings of Jesus. This document, too, disappeared from the annals of history. We know the document existed from the early days of the Christian movement. The bishops and leaders of the Death Tradition, in their communications with each other, mention it often, always in a negative manner. Either by neglect or intention, all known copies of this document also disappeared. If not for a quirk of fate and the good fortune of an Egyptian farmer, this book would still be lost to history.

In December of 1946, a local peasant went out to the cliffs that skirt the Nile, near the city of Nag Hammadi in Egypt. He came across an earthenware jar filled with ancient treatises. Among them was a copy of this ancient document from the Life Tradition of Christianity.

It turned out to be a collection of the sayings of Jesus, similar to the Sayings Gospel Q. No one knows who compiled this list of the sayings of Jesus, but in the opening sentence it describes itself as a revelation to Jesus' disciple Thomas. Hence, it was named The Gospel of Thomas.

Interestingly, most of the sayings of Jesus found in Thomas are also found in the Sayings Gospel Q. Like the Q Gospel, Thomas contains no information about the life or death of Jesus, nor does it contain any references to a resurrection. It also does not attribute to Jesus any exalted status or titles. The importance of the Gospel of Thomas is that it provides us with a second, independent early source of the sayings of Jesus, each composed in the wisdom pattern of the Life Tradition.

The Result of the Discovery of These Two Documents

The discovery in Germany in the middle of the 19th century that a sayings gospel existed, plus the discovery in Egypt 100 years later of a second sayings gospel, provides the first concrete evidence of a Life Tradition existing among the first followers of Jesus. Previously, Christianity had been considered to have had only one tradition: Paul's version of the Death Tradition. We now know there were two equally valid traditions within the early Christian movement.

These two collections of the sayings of Jesus are the earliest evidence we have of his actual teachings. They can be read by anyone, enabling us to develop a new understanding of him, as he was perceived by his first followers in Galilee. The existence of these two documents provides us with new possibilities to imagine a different kind of Christianity, a Christianity that existed from the earliest days of the movement. This new look at Christianity's early history enables us to know our present situation is neither inevitable nor unchangeable. We now have two sources containing the original sayings and parables of Jesus.

Note: In Appendix A you will find a listing of all the original sayings and parables of Jesus of Nazareth, as determined by the biblical scholars of the Jesus Seminar.

CHAPTER NINETEEN

The Danger of the Death Tradition

As we have noted, the version of the Death Tradition begun by Paul became the only version to have survived intact through these 2,000 years. Paul taught that Jesus was the Messiah and Son of God who would be returning soon in Paul's own lifetime to establish a new kingdom here on Earth, a kingdom of peace and happiness for believers. This kingdom included a resurrection from the dead of those who have been on God's side.

The Fatal Flaw of the Death Tradition

After Paul died, and the expected return of Jesus Christ never happened, the members of his churches began to question the whole concept. They started thinking surely they were going to be rewarded for being faithful to God, if not in some kingdom that may or may not come, then certainly at death they would spend eternity in heaven with Jesus and God.

But what about the people who are not believers in Jesus Christ as the Son of God? If the believers are going to be rewarded, then certainly the non-believers are going to be punished. Here begins the fatal flaw of the Death Tradition. The leaders set up a sharp dualistic point of view. You are either in or out. One spends eternity being rewarded in heaven or punished in hell, and the dividing line is what one believes about Jesus Christ. In their minds, the believers are the good people who deserve to go to heaven, while the rest are the bad people who deserve to spend eternity in hell.

In its infancy, the leaders of the Death Tradition also created an angry, judgmental, punishing image of God to carry out the job of sending people to hell. Tragically, this image of the divine has held sway throughout Christianity's bloody history and continues to this day.

The whole Death Tradition is founded on the dualistic concept that things are either right or wrong, good or evil, with no room for anything in between. This view removes any ability to question or to compromise. The Death Tradition is adamant that its version of Christianity is the only correct religion in the world. This kind of certainty leads to strident dogmatism that dismisses the views of others as wrong or dangerous or both. The supposed infallibility of its religion prompts fear and anger when any person or institution challenges or contradicts its beliefs. This fear of the "other" generated in the followers of the Death Tradition has resulted in unimaginable suffering and death throughout the centuries.

The danger in this kind of religious certainty is that it encourages believers to feel they are morally superior to non-believers and are thus justified in treating them as lesser beings. Believing they are God's chosen people leads to the concept that the end justifies the means, a concept that any means are justified to maintain and spread their religious beliefs. As we have seen, the illusion that "God is on our side" fueled a sense of superiority and justified the Crusades, the Inquisition, the torture and enslavement of indigenous peoples, and other actions that have been dangerous and deadly for humanity, even to this day.

Substitutionary Atonement

The central doctrine of the Death Tradition is the teaching that Jesus Christ, by his death upon the cross, was punished in place of all humanity as an atonement for the sins of every human being. Sometimes referred to as substitutionary atonement, his death appeased God's anger toward humanity.

This theory has focused on worshipping Jesus as a Savior instead of following him and his teachings. He became a heavenly figure who paid a brief visit to earth for the purpose of dying for the sins of humanity. Then he left and returned to heaven.

133

The doctrine of substitutionary atonement is not just a theological or academic issue. The teaching has also contributed to the narrow focus of the American criminal justice system on punishment for bad behavior instead of on rehabilitation. The idea is that if someone has been wronged, the person or persons who wronged him needs to suffer and must pay. This approach, which puts the emphasis on punishment, has resulted in a broken system that destroys individuals and families and harms all of us.

At this writing, the United States imprisons more people on a per capita basis than any other nation. With less than 5% of the world's population, we have 25% of the world's prisoners. About 2.3 million people are incarcerated right now with another 4.9 million previously incarcerated. Each person incarcerated creates far-reaching consequences for families, friends, and the larger community. Spouses are left without a mate and breadwinner, children grow up without fathers or mothers, and communities lose the taxes and other contributions of gainfully employed individuals. The label and stigma most often follow those convicted for the rest of their lives, often denying them all but the most menial, low-paying jobs. Statistics show that children of an incarcerated parent have a 50% chance of being incarcerated themselves. (https://www.prisonpolicy.org /reports/pie2020.html)

The U.S. spends $80 billion *per year* on the direct costs of incarceration. The ancillary costs—welfare, social services, mental health, etc.--are estimated at 8 to 10 times that. Yet, even our best prisons are primarily warehouses, and the worst are institutions of violence and wide-spread human suffering. Many leave prison more bitter and broken than when they entered, still lacking even the most basic skills that would enable them to become successful citizens. It is no wonder that the recidivism rate in America hovers around 70%. The Death Tradition underlies American culture and is responsible for this situation. The Death Tradition's emphasis on harsh judgment and punishment robs all of us and perpetuates the very problems we would all like to solve. Only when our nation abandons this failed approach and commits to a society based on love and restorative justice will things change.

Individualism

The doctrine of substitutionary atonement is preoccupied with individual salvation, defined as going to heaven after death. This ideology contributes to the excessive individualism that pervades the American way of life. It is difficult to care about the common good when all that counts is where one will spend eternity. In the whole process, the way of living Jesus taught becomes secondary to the overriding desire to reach heaven through belief.

Over the centuries, Christian teachers and preachers have defined Christianity almost entirely in individualistic terms while ignoring larger social issues. Care for the earth, climate change, health care, as well as social and economic inequality were either ignored or opposed. This emphasis on the individual and where that person might spend eternity harms both the individual and society. It leads to an unhealthy self-centeredness, causing one to be more concerned about his or her own good, often to the exclusion of others and the common good. If individuals lack connection, empathy, and compassion for others, social problems are sure to develop.

The Divine Christ Overshadows Jesus the Teacher

As previously noted In Part Two, the Gospel of John presents a different view of Jesus than the synoptic gospels of Mark, Matthew, and Luke. In John's gospel, Jesus is pictured as the royal divine, kingly Christ. In the other three gospels Jesus is presented as a compassionate, loving teacher and guide for how to live in this world. The Death Tradition has selected the Gospel of John as its authority on Jesus.

Many members and leaders of the churches of the Death Tradition have a hard time understanding Jesus as a teacher. He is instead only the Savior, the necessary sacrifice for our atonement. It is as if Jesus wasted his time for three years with his parables and sayings teaching humanity how to live a life of well-being and happiness in community with one another upon this earth. If all that matters is that Jesus provides a

135

pathway to heaven, we will not have much concern about what happens here on our earth.

This almost exclusive concentration on Jesus as the divine Savior and Son of God often ignores or overshadows the wise teachings of Jesus and has enabled the Death Tradition churches to define Jesus in any manner they wish. The loving acceptance of every human being becomes secondary to salvation. They can focus on his divinity and sacrificial substitutionary death. "Christ" becomes an empty canvas on which church leaders can paint any picture they choose. They can ignore Jesus' compassionate life and teachings of love, forgiveness, and care for one another, including "the least of these," and can gloss over the inconvenient teachings of Jesus, such as "Do not judge" and "Love your enemies," the Sermon on the Mount, and the parable of the Good Samaritan. Christ can become a condemning, finger-pointing judge who just happens to have the same prejudices and biases as do the leaders of the Death Tradition.

It may seem that currently the Death Tradition has an iron grip on Christianity and American society. Despite that appearance, there is a new reality that is unfolding right before our eyes.

CHAPTER TWENTY

A New Day for the Life Tradition

Looking back to the beginnings of Christianity we can see the human person, Jesus of Nazareth, was ignored by the Death Tradition of Christianity as it competed against its rivals—the pagan gods and goddesses of Greece and Rome, the popular Epicureanism, and the Life Tradition followers of Jesus. That competition was won by the Death Tradition when in the 4th century it became the official religion of the Roman Empire, resulting in a literalistic interpretation of Jesus as the divine Savior and Son of God, with devastating effects for humanity. With the advent of the modern world and modern science and knowledge, we now have the tools to rediscover Epicureanism and save Jesus from being controlled by the Death Tradition.

The Modern Era is relatively recent in human history. As previously noted, it first began to surface in the 14th and 15th centuries with the Renaissance in Europe. It blossomed in the 16th and 17th centuries with the Enlightenment, as scientists, philosophers, and other free thinkers asserted the right to think for themselves. Reason and common sense replaced the church's faith-based and fear-based domination of human thought. Prior to the Renaissance and the Enlightenment, people thought in pre-scientific terms. Their stories could include gods and goddesses, demons and devils, miracles, and other supernatural events. They would not question the validity of the story; the story was real for them, and that was all that mattered.

Today we live in the Modern Era, the age of science, reason, and common sense. We use objective measurements to separate reality from fantasy. When we read or hear an account of an event, we expect it to be factually truthful. We cannot escape this fact-based way of knowing, a way of thinking unknown to people in the pre-modern era. In the pre-modern time new knowledge, such as evolution, was judged to be true or false by whether it agreed with the Bible or some other ancient text or belief. Today the ancient text is judged by its conformity to present scientific knowledge. For example, a person walking on water as Buddha and Jesus are said to have done, or a virgin birth as has been claimed for Plato, Alexander the Great, Jesus, Roman Emperors, and other heroic figures of the past, does not conform to our modern understanding of how the world operates.

Today, humanity has moved beyond the time of being anti-science and anti-intellectual. We now determine truth by observable facts, not by whether it agrees with ancient religious texts. We today can never enter the world of the pre-modern era or think the way they thought. They could believe, for example, the Bible, Talmud, Koran, or other ancient religious documents came directly from their god and thus were sacred and infallible. Today we realize an ancient scripture was important and sacred to its followers, but we also know all human documents were written by humans for humans, and therefore are imperfect and certainly not infallible.

Humanity's central question today is also different from that of the pre-modern era. The primary concern for the younger generations is not "How can I be saved and get into heaven when I die?" The issue today is, "How can I live a happy, fulfilling, and meaningful life on this earth?" In the Modern Era many people are not focused on an afterlife; they want a life well-lived, a life that in some small way will make a difference in this world.

Rather than speculating about an unknown afterlife, people are focusing on the value of the present life they do know. There is a deep yearning for wisdom on how to live a fulfilling life in this world. This shift from the afterlife to this life is a major change in human consciousness, a shift the Death Tradition seemingly fails to recognize and continues to fight against.

This movement into the modern world has resulted in many human rights and personal freedoms not known in the pre-modern world. The rise of democracy and the freedom from control by monarchs and dictators have emerged since the period of the Enlightenment. The abolishment of slavery, as well as equal rights for women, the LBGTQ community, and people of various ethnic backgrounds are all advancements seen now in the Modern Era.

This does not mean the modern world is a kind of utopian existence. It is far from being ideal and beyond criticism. There is much more that needs to be accomplished in the modern world. Difficult choices remain to be made for the future of humanity and our planet.

Sadly, some leaders of the Death Tradition have perceived the focus on this life as the enemy of Christianity. It has become customary within the Death Tradition to view the modern culture as an assault on God and their version of the faith. The tradition has been involved in numerous "culture wars" against any progressive movements within our society. The Death Tradition has often been self-absorbed in maintaining its power and its privileged position within the nation.

What the modern world needs now are leaders with a philosophy and a faith to give it moral guidance for the future. Fortunately, there is some good news. The opportunity is now available for the emergence of both Epicureanism and the Life Tradition of Jesus the teacher.

The Withering Away of the Death Tradition

Whether they realize it, the churches of the Death Tradition are withering away. The 2019 survey of the American religious landscape by the Pew Research Center found that the fastest growing religion today is the "Nones." These are the people who respond to polls by indicating they are not affiliated with any religious group or tradition. They account for more than twenty-five percent of the population, making them the largest "religious" group in the country.

In April 2019 under the headline "Church Membership in US Plummets," the Associated Press cited a Gallup Poll showing that the percentage of U.S. adults who belong to a church or other religious institution had plunged by twenty percentage points over the previous two decades.

Furthermore, about forty percent of those under thirty give the answer to pollsters as "nones." They include many young people who want spirituality in their lives but have no interest in a religion focused on life after death instead of improving life on earth for everyone.

There are many causes for this decline in traditional religion. Among them is the belief of many young people that Christianity is a negative influence on social issues, such as LGBTQ rights, economic inequality, and climate change. According to Dr. Nancy Ackerman, professor of sociology at Boston University School of Theology, *"We see young adults who are overwhelmingly on the progressive side of sexuality and overwhelmingly not sitting still for sexual abuse of all kinds. When they see religious authorities who aren't on the right side of that, they are more likely to say, 'I'm done.' "*

The Rev. Adam Hamilton, United Methodist pastor of the Church of the Resurrection in Leawood, Kansas, states, *"Three out of four millennials who live in the U.S. support same-sex marriage and do not want to be a part of a church that makes their friends feel like second-class citizens."*

The Roman Catholic Church, as well as some of the Protestant denominations of the Death Tradition, still insist on a male-only clergy and a top-down patriarchal institutional structure representing a kind of male dominance that civil society has moved beyond. Most people in developed countries no longer embrace the idea that women are inferior to men.

There is a growing distrust of religious leaders who enrich themselves or are involved in financial or sexual scandals. The child abuse scandals within the Catholic Church and among some Protestant clergy add to that mistrust.

People today understand it is possible to live a moral or spiritual life or both without being religious or belonging to a church. Each person is free to choose their own way of living, so long as no harm is done to others.

If the Death Tradition is losing its viability, what remains from traditional Christianity? What remains in the modern world are human values such as love, justice, compassion, equality, human rights, and freedom. These are values that can be appreciated and cherished by each person, regardless of religious beliefs. These are values that grew out of the teachings of Epicurus and Jesus.

Summary

The Death Tradition has carried Christianity along for almost 2,000 years. Without the Death Tradition we may not have had any kind of Christianity. I believe we should honor and appreciate the Death Tradition and its vital role in maintaining the faith through these years. Perhaps humanity in the pre-modern era needed authoritarian political and religious leaders. Democracy, human rights, and freedom of thought were not realities in that era. Humanity may not have been ready for the Life Tradition teachings of Jesus. In one sense, Jesus may have been ahead of his time. Prior to the Modern Era, humanity may have needed belief in a supernatural deity who intervenes from time to time in this world. Those days have passed. It is increasingly obvious in the modern world that the Death Tradition and its theology are becoming outmoded.

Today there are many varieties of the Death Tradition in our world, including conservative, fundamental, evangelical, and various mainline denominations and independent churches. The more extreme versions are often characterized by anger and hostility, harsh language and combativeness, by culture wars and pessimism, as well as the claim to be the one and only true religion in the world, superior to all others.

There are also some more moderate expressions of the Death Tradition who try to hold onto both traditions at once. It is a delicate balancing act, often resulting in a tug of war between those who seek a more inclusive and socially committed church and those who want to retain the old order and often divisive approach of that belief. The battle usually moves in the direction of the Death Tradition with its one-sided emphasis on the divine Savior and Son of God who died on the cross so individuals who believe in him can enter heaven in the afterlife. The life and teachings of Jesus are relegated to second-class status, if even remembered at all.

Today we are faced with a fundamental choice that determines whether we humans can live together or not. Any political or religious system can join us together or tear us apart, depending on which of these paths it supports. If the Death Tradition continues with its "us versus them" religious and political mentality, it will tear our nation apart, and will keep our world in a state of conflict and mistrust. The stakes are high.

PART FIVE

The Art of Wellbeing and Happiness

Happiness is our only good.

The place to be happy is here.

The time to be happy is now.

The way to be happy is to make others so.

Robert Ingersoll, American orator and writer

Introduction to Part Five

I conclude this book by examining the connection between the ancient wisdom of Epicurus and Jesus and the findings about happiness based on the latest scientific discoveries. These teachings are for both the religious and the non-religious and can make a difference in each person's life.

In the Declaration of Independence, Thomas Jefferson proclaimed "the pursuit of happiness" as one of the inalienable rights of humanity. But the real question we must ask ourselves: Is the pursuit of happiness a worthwhile goal?

To answer that question, we start with one basic fact that unites all humankind—the desire for happiness. Awareness of this common desire

143

creates a bond with others and fosters a desire to work together to achieve mutual happiness, because one cannot be happy if those around that person are not. This feeling of mutuality encourages peace, acceptance, and joy. In their wisdom Epicurus and Jesus each eliminated the fear of an angry and vengeful God and taught that the way to happiness is through unconditional love of ourselves and others.

Those who study wellbeing and happiness today tell us it is deeply rooted in our view of ourselves and our relationship to others. I will cover a range of contemporary issues, from individual happiness and wellbeing, to family matters, community life, and social issues of the day. We will learn how the surprising connection between Jesus, Epicurus and the Science of Happiness can change everything in our personal lives and our societal life together.

CHAPTER TWENTY-ONE

The Science of Happiness

Over the last 30 years scientists, psychologists, and other researchers have been studying what makes us happy and how happiness affects both the individual and those around that individual. Because it is a recent development, many people are surprised to learn there really is a Science of Happiness.

The scientific study of happiness began in the late 1980's, when a Hungarian-American psychologist by the name of Mihaly Csikszentmihalyi recognized and named the psychological concept of flow, a state in which people are so involved in an activity that nothing else seems to matter; the experience is so enjoyable that people continue to do it at great cost, for the sheer sake of doing it.

The study of happiness is sometimes referred to as 'positive psychology.' In 1998, positive psychology began as a new domain of psychology when Martin Seligman chose it as the theme for his term as president of the American Psychological Association. It is a reaction against past practices, which have tended to focus on "mental illness" and emphasized maladaptive behavior and negative thinking. Today, major universities, including Harvard, Yale, Stanford, Berkley, UNC Chapel Hill, The University of Pennsylvania, and others, are engaged in research on the science of happiness. Their findings are documented in numerous books and papers, some of which are listed in the bibliography. These are not just more "self-help" articles and books. They arise out of careful scientific assessment and evaluation of the Art of Wellbeing and Happiness.

Why does the scientific study of happiness matter? It matters because happiness is one of the most important dimensions of living for the individual and because it makes for a better, healthier, and stronger society. You may not be surprised to learn the science reinforces the ancient wisdom of Epicurus and Jesus.

The researchers in the Science of Happiness describe wellbeing and happiness as "feeling that your life is good, meaningful, and worthwhile." Their research reveals that happiness has many benefits on both the individual and social level. Happy people are healthier and live longer, are not self-absorbed, have time to care about others, are more creative, charitable, and helpful to others, have more friends, and are more generous. Happy people, the facts clearly show, are flourishing people and contribute to the happiness and wellbeing of others. People who have a happy outlook on life add value to every level of life: families, neighborhoods, workplaces, communities, nations, and the globe.

What Determines Happiness

The overriding question now is: What enables some people to experience wellbeing and happiness and others not? Is it money? An active social life? A happy family or marriage? An expensive car? A nice house? A successful career? Researchers have developed the following simple equation indicating which factors influence happiness and by how much:

Your enduring level of happiness equals:

Your genetic set-point (50%) + External circumstances (10%) + Intentional Activity (40%).

Note that genetics govern 50% of our happiness, something that we are incapable of changing. The results of major events, whether they are positive or negative, affect our basic level of happiness for a relatively short period of time. In her book, *Happy for No Reason,* Science of Happiness researcher Marci Shimoff refers to a famous study that tracked people who had won the lottery, which would seem to produce great happiness. Within a year, however, these lucky winners returned to approximately the same level of happiness they had before their windfall. Surprisingly, the same was true for people who had suddenly become paraplegic. Within a year or so of being disabled, they also returned to their original happiness level.

The second factor that influences our enduring level of happiness is external circumstances. According to the experts, our external circumstances actually make up only 10% of our happiness quotient. Most people believe things like money, possessions, promotions, etc. are the keys to happiness. Research reveals this is not true. In her book, *The How of Happiness,* Sonja Lyubomirsky, distinguished professor in the Department of Psychology at the University of California, Riverside, explains:

> *Although you may find it hard to believe, whether you drive to work in a Lexus hybrid or a battered truck, whether you are young, old, or have had wrinkle-removing plastic surgery, whether you live in a frigid or balmy climate — your chances of being happy and becoming happier are pretty much the same.*

This phenomenon occurs because of how we react over time to changes in our circumstances. At first, we react strongly positively or negatively, but eventually our initial reactions subside, and we return to our set level of happiness. We may be exhilarated by the purchase of a new car, a new home, or a promotion at work, but soon the thrill wears off and we return to our previous level of happiness.

Many people spend their entire lives searching for happiness by changing their external circumstances. There is always more money to be made, more possessions to be bought, more success to be sought. Research shows that such a life is chasing an illusion and the best way to find happiness is to get off the treadmill.

That brings us to the third and most critical part of the equations: your intentional activities. This is the part of the equation over which you have control. What you think and what you do are major factors in determining the quality of your happiness. When researchers compared happy people with those who are unhappy, they found the main difference (other than genetics) is in what these people do in their daily lives. They identified many activities and strategies that have been proven to increase people's level of happiness. They found that the key to happiness lies not in changing your circumstances, such as seeking money, fame, or status, (which is usually impractical) and not in changing your genetic makeup (which is impossible), but in changing your intentional activities.

It is these strategies that make up the rest of this book. Along with the combined wisdom of Epicurus and Jesus, the Science of Happiness shows us the keys to enduring wellbeing and happiness.

CHAPTER TWENTY-TWO

The Compassionate Life

Though Epicurus did not use the word "compassion" in his teachings, he made it his goal to *"have love and happiness go dancing around the world."* He teaches us to care not just for ourselves but for all human beings.

Jesus knew that a life of happiness and living well was to be built on the foundation of compassion for others. Jesus lived what he taught. The gospels show him practicing compassion for all, regardless of their station in life. He reached out to prostitutes, lepers, the poor, the disadvantaged, young children, those who were hungry, those who were grieving, and even those who were denounced as traitors for collecting taxes for the Romans. He made compassion a hallmark of his life and his teachings.

He based his call for compassionate living on his understanding of God and encouraged his listeners to act in the same manner as this loving God when he says, *"Be compassionate as God is compassionate."* (Luke 6:36). Continuing his pattern of teaching from nature, Jesus noted we can discern that God is compassionate toward everyone, and treats everyone equally, regardless of their behavior, by observing this lesson from nature:

> *God causes the sun to rise on both the bad and the good and sends rain on both the just and the unjust.* (Matthew 5:45)

It is obvious God provides sun and rain for everyone, without judging people's behavior. The God of Jesus is a God of compassion and love.

Note that Jesus did not say "have compassion," but to "be compassionate." It is all too easy to simply have the feeling of compassion, which is similar to feelings of pity or sorrow for someone. Those feelings may or may not lead one to act on behalf of another. Jesus teaches that it is important to act on those feelings, to be compassionate.

Love Changes Everything

Love is the foundation for everything Jesus taught. A key problem with the way many practice Christianity is that they put much effort and time into the mechanics of religion rather than focusing attention on treating others with compassion and love. The one group Jesus criticized were the Jewish scribes and Pharisees who focused their religious endeavors on trying to be "right". Jesus said to them:

> Woe to you, scribes and Pharisees, For you tithe mint, dill, and cumin, and have neglected the weightier matters of the law: justice and mercy and faith...You strain out a gnat but swallow a camel. (Matthew 23:23)

Jesus spent his ministry teaching people how to live as better human beings rather than teaching humankind how to be more religious and holy. A prime example of his approach to religion is his teaching regarding the sabbath. One of the Ten Commandments in the Old Testament is, *"Remember the sabbath, and keep it holy."* In Jesus' time the above-mentioned scribes and Pharisees developed dozens and dozens of rules about keeping the Sabbath holy. These numerous requirements imposed many burdens upon the common people of Israel. Mark 2:23-27 reports an incident when Jesus is confronted by the Pharisees about his disciples plucking heads of grain to eat on the Sabbath. Jesus responds to their criticism by saying to them, *"The sabbath was made for humankind, not humankind for the sabbath."* The sabbath was created as a day of rest and refreshment for the benefit of humanity, not as a day to be burdened by a variety of rules and requirements. Religion exists, in Jesus' teaching, to enhance the wellbeing of human life upon this earth, not as a means to judge and condemn human beings or try to control their behavior.

Luke recounts an interchange between a potential follower who asks Jesus about inheriting eternal life. Jesus answers with the two great commandments from the Hebrew scriptures: *Love God with all your heart, mind, soul, and strength* and *Love your neighbor as yourself.*

Jesus followed this response by telling the parable of the Good Samaritan, which demonstrates the fact that love means action. As you read this story, keep in mind the Samaritans and the Jews were longtime bitter enemies of one another. The Jews regarded the Samaritans as low-life half-breeds and the Samaritans saw the Jews as haughty, mean-spirited people. Jesus is telling the story to fellow Jews.

> *There was a man going from Jerusalem down to Jericho, when he fell into the hands of robbers. They stripped him, beat him up and went off, leaving him half-dead. Now by coincidence a priest was going down that road; and when he caught sight of the man, he went out of his way to avoid him. In the same way, a Levite when he came to the place, he took one look at him and crossed the road to avoid him. But this Samaritan who was traveling that way came to where he was and was moved to pity at the sight of him. He went up to him and bandaged his wounds, pouring olive oil and wine on them. He hoisted him onto his own animal, brought him to an inn, and looked after him. The next day he took out two silver coins, which he gave to the innkeeper, and said, 'Look after him, and on my way back I'll reimburse you for any extra expense you have had.' (Luke 10:30-37)*

Here Jesus demonstrates the value of treating each other with great compassion and shows that we can learn to love those who seem different from us. He is breaking down the distinction between "us" and "them." There is only "us." We may *seem* different to each other, but the truth is we are all one.

As with all the teachings of Jesus, there is a personal, social, and political dimension to his call for us to be compassionate. He reminds us to follow the golden rule: *Do unto others as you would have them do unto you.* One can do this personally, through direct action, or indirectly, by supporting charities and government policies designed to help those who need it.

The message of the Golden Rule can be found in all the world's major religions.

Do Not Judge

Another factor in living a happy life is to refrain from judging others because each of us is imperfect. Jesus provided this teaching regarding the issue of passing judgment on others:

> *Why do you notice the sliver in your friend's eye, but overlook the timber in your own? How can you say to your friend, 'Let me get the sliver out of your eye" when there is that timber in your own eye? You phony, first take the timber out of your own eye and then you'll see well enough to remove the sliver from your friend's eye.'* (Matthew 7:3-5)

In this vivid and humorous image, Jesus points out the folly of standing in judgment of others when we each have our own shortcomings. Jesus did not provide any loopholes here. Judging is always harmful, for oneself and for others. When we judge others, we fall into the trap of insisting that other people behave as we want them to. We develop negative feelings and actions toward others. Judging keeps us stuck and makes us miserable.

Social media and advertising encourage us to continually compare ourselves with others, to make judgments about whether we are ahead or behind. We end up spending time and energy worrying about whether people like us and whether we "measure up." The Science of Happiness has much to say about the damage that results. When we judge we are ahead, we sometimes look down on others and treat them with contempt. Judging we are behind leads to low self-esteem and resentment. Either way, these feelings result in unhappiness for one's self or for others.

The cure for judging and comparing is to practice compassion. Compassion is non-judgmental, toward one's self and others. When we practice compassion toward ourselves, we accept ourselves as we are. We may want to grow and improve in certain areas of our life, but we don't compare ourselves to others in order to define who we are. When we practice compassion toward others, we take delight in their happiness and rejoice in their success and good fortune rather than envying or resenting it in any way. Doing so increases our own happiness and the happiness of those around us. Jesus made it clear. In every aspect of life, do not pass judgment.

Summary

Modern studies have shown that we humans are wired to be compassionate. Early humans lived in an extremely difficult and dangerous world. The unpredictable forces of nature and the strength and speed of wild animals put their existence in continual jeopardy. Their very survival depended upon their ability to cooperate with each other. Compassion promoted social harmony which was and is an essential ingredient for pursuing a happy and productive life.

Karen Armstrong, noted author of numerous books on religion, suggests that compassion is like driving a car. You do not learn to drive by reading the owner's manual. You get behind the wheel and get into traffic. Likewise, compassion comes as we learn to put it into practice. We make progress by modifying our behavior and learning to think and act toward others in accordance with the golden rule.

The Science of Happiness confirms that insight. The good news is that you can train your brain to be happier. Happiness is a life-long process. It takes practice and it takes work, but the pursuit of true happiness through compassion brings great benefits.

The Dalia Lama expressed it this way,

> *If you want others to be happy, practice compassion. If you want to be happy, practice compassion.*

CHAPTER TWENTY-THREE

Family and Friends

Epicurus and Jesus built communities of friends who lived cooperatively, voluntarily sharing their food and goods. It is understandable, then, that each would focus on friends over family.

In the world of Epicurus, and three centuries later in the world of Jesus, the family had an importance that is difficult to imagine for those of us in the contemporary world. The family was not a nuclear family consisting only of parents and their children. It was an extended family, consisting of parents, children, grandparents, brothers, sisters, aunts, uncles, and other relatives. People lived in these extended families throughout their lifetime rather than growing up and leaving home. Each family was, in a real sense, a separate tribe or a clan within a tribe.

The family was the primary social and economic unit in society. It was the source of one's status. However, it could also be constraining. The family was strongly patriarchal, with authority controlled entirely by men, especially the elders. The father was the absolute ruler of the family. There was great pressure to obey the dictates of the father and to remain within the family structure. To leave the family was to lose one's status and position and risk becoming a nobody. Yet, both Epicurus and Jesus chose this route, each one breaking free from the constraints of his own family ties.

When Epicurus left his hometown to pursue his philosophical career, as far as we know, he never returned home. There is no evidence in his extensive writings that he ever mentioned family relationships. On the other hand, he had much to say about the importance of friendships. Epicurus believed friendship is so important for living a happy life that it should not be left to chance. One should make the building of friendship an integral part of one's life. He says,

> Of all the preparations that wisdom makes for the blessedness of the complete life, by far the most precious is the acquisition of friendship.

At a time when there was no Social Security or pensions for the later years of life, and the legal system was often corrupt and stacked against the ordinary person, Epicurus advised his followers to seek peace and safety through friendship. He believed friends provide one another the greatest security, whereas a life without friends is solitary and full of difficulties.

Epicurus taught that friendship is to be intentionally and diligently cultivated, saying,

> We ought to look around for people to eat and drink with, before we look for something to eat and drink; to feed without a friend is the life of a lion or a wolf.

Just knowing one has friends to count on in the emergencies of life enables a person to live a happy and tranquil life. For there to be friendship, Epicurus wrote, there must be trust between friends, and friends must love one another as well as they love themselves. Friendship means having the courage to stand with or even sacrifice for a friend in a time of need or danger.

Epicurus elevated friendship to one of the highest priorities among the virtues. He ranked friendship to be valued equally with wisdom:

> The truly noble man concerns himself chiefly with wisdom and friendship, of which the one is an understandable good and the other immortal.

Epicurus highly valued the blessing of friendship, as shown in these poetic words: *Friendship dances around the world proclaiming to us all to rouse ourselves to give thanks.*

To Epicurus, love and friendship were interchangeable terms. This love of others extends to embrace all humankind. In another poetic phrase he says, *"Love goes dancing round and round the inhabited earth, veritably shouting to us all to awake to the blessedness of the happy life."*

Epicurus and his disciples were noted for their friendly attitude toward everyone. They accepted each person for who they were, not for what station in life they had achieved. This friendly, open, egalitarian spirit greatly enhanced their ability to carry the message of Epicureanism to people in a wide variety of cultural settings.

The English words "friendship" and "love" are encapsulated in the Greek word *philia*. It refers to a friendly love that begins with a circle of immediate friends, which extends to include all humanity. Epicurus was known as a person of love, compassion, and friendship for all humankind, and he made sharing that love with others a hallmark of his philosophical school.

The gospels show Jesus prioritized friendships as well. His disciples were his closest friends, traveling with him as he goes to the villages throughout Galilee. His contemporaries criticized him for spending too much time with his friends, plus they condemned his choice of friends.

The gospels portray Jesus expressing a surprising preference for friends over family, as described in Matthew 12:46-50:

> *While he was still speaking to the crowds, his mother and his brothers were standing outside, wanting to speak to him. Someone told him, "Look, your mother and your brothers are standing outside, wanting to speak to you." But to the one who had told him this, Jesus replied, "Who are my mother, and who are my brothers?" And pointing to his disciples, he*

said, *"Here are my mother and my brothers!"* (Matthew 12:46-50)

Perhaps Jesus was following the guidance of the wisdom tradition as expressed in Proverbs:

> *A friend loves at all times, and kinsfolk are born to share adversity.* (17:17)

> *Do not forsake your friend... better is a neighbor who is nearby than kindred who are far away.* (27:10)

Like Epicurus, Jesus focused his attention on the shared communal lifestyle that enables a person to find peace of mind and a sense of safety. In an environment where a villager could be arrested and thrown into prison by the Roman authorities at any moment, this new communal family of friends offered security and the assurance of help in time of need.

In America, rugged individualism has traditionally been valued over community and the common good. The United States is the most individualistic country in modern Western culture. Generations have been taught to believe the only way to be successful is to make it on one's own, which is thought to be the natural state of being human. Our society is built on competition and personal achievement, leading many to feel vulnerable and lonely. This has also resulted in a vast gulf in wealth, with a relative few who are extremely rich and large numbers who are grindingly poor. The top 1% own more wealth than the bottom 80%.

Friends can literally save one's life. A variety of studies and tests from around the world now demonstrate that warm social ties and secure relationships can boost immune functions, improve the quality of life, and lower the risk of contracting a variety of diseases. People who have extensive networks of friendships are better able to fight off disease and trauma than those who do not. A connected life is not only a contented life; it is also a healthy life.

Certified Human Life Coach Hamish W. Ziegler pinpoints the key ingredient to happiness:

> *According to a seven-decade, ongoing study by Harvard University on happiness, after painstaking examination of families, their blood types, their work and dreams from childhood to old age, from alcoholics to a President, the single most important key to human happiness was found to be deep, meaningful relationships...Imagine that each deep relationship we have is the foundation of our own happiness. Because it is.*

CHAPTER TWENTY-FOUR

Enemies and Difficult People

Every human being has some difficult people in their life. In dealing with enemies and difficult people, Epicurus advises:

> *That man has best forestalled the feeling of insecurity from outside who makes relations friendly where possible, where impossible, at least neutral, and where even this is impossible, avoids contacts.*

While Epicurus advised his followers to seek to live peaceably with all persons, even enemies, Jesus intensified the guidance regarding friendship by telling his followers they should learn to:

> *Love your enemies! If you love those who love you, what merit is there in that? After all, even sinners love those who love them.* (Luke 6: 27, 35)

This is an honest statement in that we will have real enemies in this world as individuals, groups, and nations. Jesus' teachings do not assume one will not have enemies; rather, he teaches people how to act when they encounter them.

The villagers he addressed certainly knew who the enemy was. First and foremost, the enemy was the Roman rulers, their ever-present military forces, and their Jewish puppets. Jesus' listeners suffered greatly at the hands of the Romans, who ruled over them with an iron fist. Jesus knows that loving one's enemies is hard work and is clearly not asking us to have loving feelings toward our enemies. He is calling on them to act in a loving manner toward those who oppressed them.

Jesus' guidance was both practical and sensible. He said:

> Do not resist an evildoer. But if anyone strikes you on the right cheek, turn the other also; and if any wants to sue you and take your coat, give your cloak as well; and if anyone forces you to go one mile, go also the second mile. (Matthew 5:39-41)

Jesus taught on openhearted attitude designed to disarm the enemy. He viewed this approach as an effective tactic to shame and confront the Roman soldiers who were the occupiers of the Jewish lands. These responses to their cruelty were ways to embarrass the enemy, reveal his hypocrisy and even force him to take a second look at his behavior, and at least question his actions. The villagers would be safer and experience greater peace through acts of kindness rather than acts of defiance or rebellion. On a larger scale, if we return ugly behavior with ugly behavior, we just escalate the animosity, and the situation continues to worsen. Jesus' teaching is not some naïve pacifism but rather a smart way to change the situation and create a more peaceful outcome to the conflict.

Hatred can never cease by hatred. Hatred can only cease by forgiveness, which is an expression of the kind of love at the heart of Jesus' teachings. Love forgives. However, it is not easy. It is much more difficult to forgive than to hold a grudge. It is much easier to carry around anger and resentment. It is, however, self-defeating. When our minds are full of those negative emotions, we are the ones who suffer, caught in the grip of this state of mind. Someone has compared carrying resentment around inside of you to taking a drink of poison with the expectation it will kill the person who has offended you.

Forgiveness is a process. It does not mean condoning a harmful action. It should never be confused with being silent toward violation or abuse. It is an inner relinquishing of resentment, which may or may not change the other person. But it will change the forgiver, and that is what counts.

160

Bernard Metzger, founder of *Sustainable First*, expressed it this way:

> *When you forgive, you in no way change the past—but you sure do change the future.*

This same principle applies on the national and international level. Our world has become a global village, so that everyone is our neighbor. It is essential that we regard everyone as a member of our village and seek to make allies of our enemies. In his book *An Open Heart: Practicing Compassion in Everyday Life,* the Dalai Lama pointed out:

> *We are now so interdependent that the concept of war has become outmoded...one-sided victory is no longer relevant. We must strive for reconciliation and always remember the interests of others. We cannot destroy our neighbors or ignore their interests! This would ultimately lead to our own suffering.*

Yes, Jesus taught the way of love, compassion, and forgiveness, even of one's enemies. On a social and political level Mahatma Gandhi, Martin Luther King, Jr., Nelson Mandela, and other advocates of nonviolent resistance learned that truth and followed the path of Jesus. Their actions are the essential core of his teaching.

CHAPTER TWENTY-FIVE

Money Matters

The correlation between Epicurus' teachings and those of Jesus can been seen quite clearly when we compare their positions on money matters. As we saw in Chapter Six, they each had much to say about the subject of wealth and the deceitfulness of riches.

Epicurus believed the delusion that greater wealth brings greater happiness is the cause of many of the problems experienced in one's daily life:

> Riches do not exhilarate us so much with their possession as they torment us with their loss.

Epicurus also made these observations about the delusion of wealth:

> We should envy no man, for good men do not deserve envy and, as for evil men, the more they prosper the more they spoil their own chance of happiness.

> By means of occupation worthy of a beast, abundance of riches is heaped up, but a miserable life results.

According to Epicurus, enough is enough and too much is nothing.

We need enough food to live, but too much food is harmful.

We need enough clothes to wear, but too much is emptiness.

We need shelter to be safe, but too much is a burden.

We need enough money to survive, but too much is a worry.

Jesus took the issue of money to a whole new level. He does not regard the love of money as simply an individual moral issue. He bases his understanding of money on his view of what God wants for human beings on this earth. He starts with his central concept, "the kingdom of God." Here the bottom line is people, not money. He pictures God's will for humankind as a place where each person is treated equally with dignity and respect. The kingdom of God is where people share their resources generously with one another, where there is no distinction between classes and race.

According to Jesus, we are faced with a stark choice:

> *No man can serve two masters; for a slave will either hate the one and love the other or be devoted to one and despise the other. You cannot serve God and mammon.* (Matthew 6:24)

The Greek word *mammon* means wealth or chasing after wealth. Choosing God over mammon means replacing valuing people based on their financial success with valuing each person simply because they are human.

Jesus also comments on the difficulty of being rich and being a member of the kingdom of God:

> *How hard it is to enter the kingdom of God! It is easier for a camel to go through the eye of a needle than for someone who is rich to enter the kingdom of God.* (Mark 10:23, 25)

Jesus' humorous graphic exaggeration of a camel trying to squeeze through the eye of a needle makes the point clearly. There is a dramatic difference, according to Jesus, between living a life of mutual compassion and care for one another and chasing after wealth.

The issue plays itself out on both social and political levels. As a nation, what do we value? Do we measure our success as a nation by our GDP or by how well we treat each person in our society? Do we organize our nation to ensure that no child goes hungry, that everyone has adequate shelter, that health care is equally available to every person in our society?

Jesus places the issue squarely before us. There is a choice, individually and as a nation--God's way (treating each person equally with compassion) or mammon (wealth and accumulating more and more).

The recent findings of the Science of Happiness confirm the wisdom of Epicurus and Jesus, reminding us of the "myth of more." This is the illusion that happiness comes when you get "more" and the list of "more" is endless: a nicer car, a bigger house, a promotion, a pay raise, a new boat, a luxury vacation, a new dress or suit, a new hairdo, and the list goes on.

Happiness researchers pretty much agree on one thing: what matters most for human wellbeing is our relationships with others. As Elizabeth Dunn and Michael Norton, authors of *Happy Money,* have noted:

> *New research shows that spending small amounts of money on others can make a difference for our own happiness. Rather than think about the different ways you can spend money on yourself to maximize your own happiness, consider investing it in others. Spending your money on others can increase your happiness even more than spending your cash on yourself.*

The authors also note:

> *Whoever said, "Money can't buy happiness" didn't know where to shop.*

The book summarizes current research on how you spend money changes how happy and satisfied you are in life. It also affects your health and wellbeing. You can increase your happiness by spending your money on experiences with people you value, rather than spending it on items that many people tend to believe will make them happy.

Experiences we share with others, rather than "stuff," tend to make us feel more connected to other people, which improves our level of wellbeing and happiness. Anything we do to make the time with friends or partners special is money well spent. Buy experiences, especially shared, unique ones that express your sense of who you are.

The advice to invest in others pays off in the form of happiness rather than cash. People feel happier after thinking about a time when they spent money on others than on themselves. It promotes happiness and has the added benefit of potentially spurring a domino effect of generosity.

It is important to remember, however, we live in a Western culture that trains us that material goods, not relationships, are what one needs to be happy. This concept has been indoctrinated in us since childhood. In this environment, it is difficult to know and trust one's better instincts regarding wealth and happiness. Valuing material possessions above all else means placing less value on ourselves and those around us.

Research by the leaders of the Science of Happiness reveals that happiness based on having more is temporary and fragile. Neither a sudden windfall nor a tragedy has a lasting effect on the happiness level of human beings. Happiness, they show us, comes from within or it may not come at all. The more one thinks happiness is about having stuff and status, the more anxious and unhappy one becomes, trapped on the economic treadmill and losing the most precious value one can have— meaningful connection to others.

All this is not to say that money is unimportant. If one is living in poverty, it is extremely difficult to have a life of wellbeing and happiness. Worrying about having the financial resources to feed one's family, pay the rent, the mortgage, or utility bills, or facing a financial disaster such as loss of a job or a health crisis, can take away one's ability to be happy.

Science of Happiness research indicates the move from poverty to simple financial stability greatly increases one's happiness level. However, financial increases beyond that level result in much smaller increases in happiness. The further up the income level one goes, the less the difference in the level of happiness.

In a recent study conducted by Michael Norton and Dan Ariely, *Building a Better America—One Wealth Quintile at a Time*, they surveyed some five thousand Americans on wealth inequality in the nation. Amazingly, Republicans and Democrats, rich and poor, show remarkable consensus in their desired distribution of wealth. They support more equal distribution of wealth but are willing to tolerate some wealth inequality.

Another study by Shigehiro Oishi, Selin Kesebir, and Ed Diener titled *Income Inequality and Happiness* finds that more even distribution of wealth is associated with greater happiness within a nation. Their research shows that a more equal distribution of money across a nation's population is associated with higher average wellbeing and happiness within that country. In other words, the overall wellbeing of the country was related to the relative equality of their inhabitant's incomes.

On an individual level and on a societal level, money matters. Epicurus sought to help people overcome the delusion of wealth and focus on human relationships. Three hundred years later Jesus joined him in that endeavor, and today those studying the Science of Happiness are confirming what they taught centuries ago.

CHAPTER TWENTY-SIX

A Simple Life

For Epicurus, the simple life is the way to happiness. He and his followers lived such a life, eating and drinking moderately. He believed that the simple life provides a sense of security; it renders the individual *"unshrinking before the inevitable vicissitudes of life"* and *"fearless in the face of Fortune."* If a person tries to live beyond or on the edge of one's means, every hiccup in life will be a threat to happiness and security. Persons who live within their means are free from worry about the unexpected difficulties that are sure to arise. He taught:

> Nature provides that everything that is necessary to life is easily obtained, and that those things which are idle or vain are difficult to possess. Simple flavors give as much pleasure as costly fare when everything that causes pain and every feeling of want is removed. Bread and water give the most extreme pleasure when someone in need eats of them. To accustom oneself, therefore, to simple and inexpensive habits is a great ingredient towards perfecting one's health and makes one free from hesitation in facing the necessary affairs of life. And when on certain occasions we fall in with more sumptuous fare, this attitude renders us better disposed towards luxuries, as we are then fearless with regard to the possibility that we may thereafter lose them.

Epicurus said of himself:

> I spit upon luxurious pleasures, not for their own sake but because of the inconveniences that follow them.

Jesus also taught his disciples the value of simple living as the pathway to a life of wellbeing and happiness. About his own life of simplicity, Jesus noted that he himself was homeless:

> *Foxes have holes, and birds of the air have nests, but the son of man [Jesus] has nowhere to lay his head. [brackets mine]* (Luke 9:58)

Perhaps the best place to clearly see the simple life Jesus advocated is in his instructions to his followers when he sent them out on their journeys to the villages of Galilee:

> *Take nothing for your journey, no staff, nor bag, nor bread, nor money – not even an extra tunic.* (Luke 9:3)

> *Take no gold, or silver, or copper in your belts, no bag for your journey, or two tunics, or sandals, or a staff.* (Matthew 10:9)

His followers went out two by two as they traveled from village to village. They depended on the traditional Mediterranean hospitality of the villagers. By traveling light, they set the example of how to live simply.

Both Jesus and Epicurus taught that a generous heart is an essential component of a simple life. Modern science confirms this. Generosity has power because it can change and enrich life in profound and long-lasting ways. As H. Jackson Brown, Jr., best known for his inspirational book *Life's Little Instruction Book,* says,

> The happiest people are not those who are getting more, but those giving more.

In our modern world, we are bombarded with constant commercials enticing us to want more money, more products, more status, a better job, a better body. If we get what we want, we feel satisfied for a brief time, but then we end up wanting more. We are conditioned to crave, to grasp, to want.

Practicing generosity frees us from the continual longing for more and focuses our attention on giving to and caring for others. The Science of Happiness has found that spending money on others brings more happiness than spending money on ourselves. And there are many other ways to give to others. We can give time, service, friendship, kindness, and love. These gifts enrich us and those to whom we give. They increase our happiness and the happiness of others. We all benefit.

A generous heart and a simple lifestyle are essential ingredients in finding a life of wellbeing and happiness. Epicurus and Jesus taught this truth, and The Science of Happiness confirms the wisdom of their teachings.

CHAPTER TWENTY-SEVEN

The Importance of Now

Epicurus taught that living in the present is the way to happiness. Today, we call this "mindfulness." This is not easy, as most spend conscious time regretting past mistakes or worrying about future events. However, with the proper perspective on the past and the future, we can learn to focus on the here and now.

Our human brains have equipped us with the ability to contemplate the past, the present, and the future. Memory is the faculty that allows us to see the past. Imagination is the brain's tool that allows us to peer into the future. Both are vital to our wellbeing and happiness, but both are flawed. Epicurus had much to say about both memory and imagination, as well as how to live mainly in the present.

THE PAST

The most common way of dwelling on the past is mulling over our mistakes or the perceived injustices done toward us. We must accept that making mistakes is a fundamental part of being human and that almost every ability we have--walking, talking, reading, writing, riding a bicycle—was learned by making mistakes. It is wise to learn from past mistakes, but it is also important to let them go. We cannot change what we or others did in the past. We can only change our attitude about what happened in the past.

Our memories are well-suited for remembering past experiences in a positive manner. It's rewarding to replay a happy event or success. Think about an event or time in the past when you were happy and fulfilled, when you felt good about life, especially your own life, and replay it in your mind. Taking time to savor these past experiences is a way to increase our happiness in the present. However, not all memories are happy ones. Some are quite painful. Epicurus teaches us to focus on remembered happy experiences, events, and interactions from the past and let go of the painful memories.

Epicurus sums up an important truth regarding the past when he says:

> Misfortune must be cured through gratitude for what has been lost (that is, the past) and the knowledge that it is impossible to change what has happened.

THE FUTURE

Our brains also equip us with the power of imagination, enabling us to develop pictures of our future. You may remember John Lennon asked us to "imagine there's no countries." He also added "it isn't hard to do." He was right. Imagination about the future does not take much effort. We are designed to think about the future.

The future is not pre-ordained, and much depends on the choices we make in the present. The healthy attitude toward the future is to know we can work toward and shape the future we want. Our brain insists on imagining the future so we can be better prepared for whatever the future may hold.

Studies have shown that a healthy anticipation of the future can greatly enhance present moments. Merely imaging the future can itself be a source of happiness and joy. People enjoy planning and thinking about an upcoming vacation trip and enjoy the anticipation of future pleasures. However, we must guard against the mistake of thinking of happiness as something that can only happen in the future when we are free of current problems.

For Epicurus, gratitude for the past and hope for the future are key to living happily. People who are discouraged about their past and pessimistic about their future are unhappy and contribute to the unhappiness of those around them. It is for this reason that the virtues of gratitude and hope are so important.

THE PRESENT

A key Epicurean teaching is that true happiness comes when we make the present moment the primary focus of our life. Epicurus teaches that the past is not available to live again, nor is happiness currently available in the unknown future. Happiness is only available in the now.

The importance of now gives a sense of urgency to life. Epicurus viewed procrastination as one of the sources of an unhappy life:

> *We are born once and we cannot be born twice but for all time must be no more; and you, thou fool, though not the master of the morrow, postpone the hour and life is frittered away in procrastination and each and every one of us goes to death with excuses on our lips.*

Acceptance of our mortality gives to the present a strong sense of urgency, for this life provides the only opportunity for action. The significance of the present is expressed by Epicurus in these poetic words:

> *He that sayeth the hour for putting philosophy into practice is not yet come or has passed by is like unto him that sayeth the hour for happiness is not yet come or is no more.*

Whatever good you mean to do, whatever love you want to express, whatever accomplishments you wish to achieve, do them now--in the present. Realizing our own mortality and the importance of the present moment overcomes the folly of procrastination.

Like Epicurus, Jesus focused on the importance of living in the present, not in some future life after death. Jesus' central teaching was a way of living in the present according to God's desires for humankind. Jesus called this the kingdom (or domain) of God, where the worth and dignity of every person is honored equally. However, in Jesus' time the Jewish people in Israel were

172

living under the brutal rule of the Roman Empire and longed for a Messiah to come and drive out the hated Romans and install God's rule in Israel. While this longing is understandable, it led to a focus on the future at the expense of the present. When Jesus was asked by the Pharisees when the domain and rule of God would come, he replied,

> You won't be able to see the coming of God's domain and rule...On the contrary, God's domain and rule is right here in your presence. (Luke 17:20-21)

The Pharisees were looking for a future event to such an extent they failed to see the opportunity that was all around them -- the opportunity to live a compassionate life, the way God wanted people to live in relationship with one another.

Jesus said to the crowds, who evidently were raising questions about the future and when the Messiah might come:

> When you see a cloud rising in the west, right away you say that it's going to rain; and so it does. And when the wind blows from the south, you say we're in for scorching heat; and we are. You phonies! You know the lay of the land and can read the face of the sky, so why don't you know how to interpret the present time. (Luke 12:54-56)

Instead of focusing on what might happen in the future, we can learn to live more fully in the present. From another perspective, the comedian Groucho Marx put it this way:

> I, not the events, have the power to make me happy today. I can choose which it will be. I'm going to be happy in it.

Happiness comes from learning to live every moment of each day with love, compassion, and gratitude, controlling what we can control and accepting what we cannot control.

It is best to live in the moment and learn as you go along, remaining open to new lessons from unexpected sources. That openness to learning new truths, new realities, new perspectives often leads to greater happiness and wellbeing in life.

Epicurus and Jesus each taught the importance of NOW. We can have gratitude for the past and hope for the future, but ultimately life is always NOW and the time to live a happy and fulfilling life is NOW.

CHAPTER TWENTY-EIGHT

Gratitude and Celebration

Epicurus and Jesus each taught the importance of gratitude and celebration.

Epicurus considered gratitude to be a chief aspect of happiness. Its opposite, ingratitude, was a chief cause of misery and unhappiness.

Epicurus noted:

> We must not spoil the enjoyment of the blessings we have by pining for those we have not, but rather reflect that these we have are among the things desirable.

Epicurus realized that ungrateful people are not only discontented but also worry about their future:

> The life of the fool is marked by ingratitude and apprehension; the drift of his thought is exclusively toward the future.

> The adage which says, "Look to the end of a long life," bespeaks a lack of gratitude for past blessings.

He proclaimed:

> The wise man alone will know true gratitude.

Epicurus also knew the importance of making celebration a part of one's life. In his writings he makes it clear the simple life does not mean asceticism. It does not involve constant denial of pleasure or a vow of poverty. What it does mean is simple eating, drinking, and living, which is the way Epicurus and his students conducted their daily lives, with one exception.

On the twentieth day of the month they would put away their philosophy studies and spend the day preparing for a sumptuous evening banquet. In addition, they would also celebrate the annual holidays of the Greek culture with festive banquet meals.

Jesus also knew the importance of connecting gratitude and celebration. He taught the villagers to have regular festive communal meals to share with one another where everyone was invited—rich or poor, adult or child, ill or healthy. These were times of joy, sharing food, drink, and conversation. They were times to set aside personal worries and concerns and come together in communal happiness. These were celebrations in and of themselves.

The gospels portray Jesus as a real flesh-and-blood human being who loved life and lived joyfully. His detractors accused him of being too much of a partier. They point out that the disciples of John the Baptist and the Pharisees both fast, but that Jesus and his disciples do not fast. Jesus responds,

> *The wedding guests cannot fast while the bridegroom is with them, can they? While they have the bridegroom with them, they cannot fast.* (Mark 2:19)

He also said:

> *To what shall I compare the people of this generation, and what are they like? They are like children sitting in the marketplace and calling to one another, "We played the flute for you, and you did not dance. We wailed, and you did not weep." For John the Baptist has come eating no bread and drinking no wine, and you say, "He has a demon"; the son of Man has come eating and drinking, and you say, "Look, a glutton and a drunkard, a friend of tax collectors and sinners.* (Luke 7:31-34)

In the Beatitudes Jesus affirms the message of joy and hope for the peasants of Galilee. The Beatitudes are found in the gospels of Matthew and Luke. Biblical scholars consider the version found in Luke to be more closely aligned with the actual teachings of Jesus. The Greek word usually translated as "blessed" can also mean "fortunate" or "happy." These three Beatitudes are found in Luke:

> *Happy (blessed) are you who are poor, for yours is the kingdom of God. Happy (blessed) are you who are hungry now, for you will be filled. Happy (blessed) are you who weep now, for you will laugh.* (Luke 6:20-21)

Jesus tells the Galilean peasants, who are suffering and competing with one another for scarce resources, that they can have a kingdom of God lifestyle in their villages, where through communal sharing there will be enough for everyone. The hungry will have ample food to eat (will be filled). Those who are grieving because they have not been able to feed their family (who weep now) will find happiness (will laugh) in this new way of living in relationship with one another. All this will happen now in their villages, where cooperating with one another beats competing against one another. That is the kingdom way.

Jesus' desire to bring happiness to people is made evident in his teaching about the Sabbath day. Mark tells the story:

> *One sabbath Jesus was going through the grain fields, and as they made their way his disciples began to pluck heads of grain. The Pharisees said to him, "Look, why are they doing what is not lawful on the sabbath?". Then he said to them, the sabbath was made for humankind, not humankind for the sabbath."* (Mark 2:23-28)

In a time when a seven-day work week was common, the sabbath was instituted as a day of rest and refreshment for everyone, including the farm animals. Over the years the Jewish religious leaders had developed many rules and regulations regarding the observance of the sabbath. Obeying these restrictions became a burden upon the people. Jesus proclaimed the principle that the sabbath was established for the benefit and happiness of humankind, not a day of laboriously following myriad rules and regulations.

Jesus also linked gratitude with celebration. In the following two parables, Jesus teaches the importance of both gratitude and celebration.

> *Is there any one of you who owns a hundred sheep and one of them gets lost, who wouldn't leave the ninety-nine in the wilderness and go after the one that got lost until he finds it? And when he finds it, he lifts it upon his shoulders, happy. Once he gets home, he invites his friends and his neighbors over, and says to them, "Celebrate with me, because I have found my lost sheep."* (Luke 15:4-6)

> *Is there any woman with ten silver coins, who if she loses one, wouldn't light a lamp and sweep the house and search carefully until she finds it? When she finds it, she invites her friends and neighbors over and says, "Celebrate with me, because I have found the silver coin I had lost."* (Luke 15 8-9)

The twin stories of the lost sheep and the lost coin each have a note of humor in them. The villagers hearing the parable of the lost sheep would immediately recognize this to be an irresponsible act by the shepherd. He abandoned the ninety-nine sheep, thereby exposing them to danger. More of the sheep may wander off or wild animals might attack the flock.

Furthermore, when he finds the lost sheep, the shepherd does not return to the ninety-nine he left in the wilderness. He takes the sheep home with him and calls his friends and neighbors to come celebrate with him over the finding of the lost sheep. In that culture, the host would normally provide the meat for the celebration, meaning he would need to slaughter the lamb he has just found. Therein lies the humor.

In the second story a woman, who is evidently a widow, has ten silver coins, representing her life's savings. She loses one, searches diligently for it, finds it, and calls her friends and neighbors to come celebrate with her.

She spends the newly found coin to throw a party to celebrate her good fortune. From a practical point of view, this does not make sense.

Both parables emphasize the joy that comes from celebrating one's gratitude with friends and neighbors. From one perspective the actions of the shepherd and the widow seem rather foolish, yet it is this very act of celebrating together that enhances the joy for everyone.

In contrast to other philosophers and religious leaders, Jesus and Epicurus focused their teachings on living a joyous life of gratitude and celebration. The Science of Happiness confirms this approach. Regularly recalling happy moments in our past with thanksgiving adds joy to the present and often dispels a negative mood. Instead of feeling we don't have enough, a grateful spirit leads to contentment and inner peace. It can be as simple as the familiar saying, "Count your blessings." This spirit spreads to those around us, enhancing our relationship to others.

Expressing gratitude toward others is a way of showing our love for and appreciation of the role they play in our lives. It makes them feel valued. Gratitude generates gratitude. People on the receiving end of gratitude often find a way to pass it along to others.

It also leads us to make healthier decisions. As Science of Happiness psychologist Sonja Lysbomursky, a professor in the Department of Psychology at the University of California, Riverside, found, people feeling gratitude make healthier food choices and are more inclined to engage in healthy exercise.

Celebration is the companion of gratitude. We celebrate birthdays, marriages, victories, promotions, and finding a lost sheep or a lost coin. While spending time and money on celebrations may seem frivolous, there is something in us that causes us to want to share these happy moments with others.

Studies in the Science of Happiness have shown that gratitude has many positive effects: People who are grateful are happier, have more energy, and are more optimistic. They are also more likely to have positive feelings and convey those feelings to others. Grateful people are more sympathetic, forgiving, and helpful. They are also less materialistic than people who are less grateful.

Finally, in his book, *The 90 Day Happiness Journal,* Prof. Detlef Beeker notes:

> *Grateful people suffer less from depression, nervousness, loneliness, envy, and neuroses.*

These are among the many advantages of gratitude and celebration. None of us can experience constant happiness or euphoria. However, if we learn the art of living a life of gratitude and celebration with others, we can find happiness in the everyday experiences of life.

We can generate feelings of gratitude. Be intentional in developing a feeling of gratitude for all the good things in your life. You could keep a daily gratitude journal in which you record three things for which you are grateful. When you start the day feeling grateful, you are more likely to feel happier throughout the rest of the day.

Epicurus and Jesus, as well as those studying the Science of Happiness, teach the value of including gratitude and celebration in one's life as an important source of wellbeing and happiness.

CHAPTER TWENTY-NINE

Fear of Death

Epicurus realized one of the great fears in the public mind of his day was the fear of death. Epicurus set himself the goal of liberating humanity from the fear of death and of reconciling us to the reality of mortality.

The first thing we can say of Epicurus' teaching about death is that he had the same view of death as traditional Judaism. Neither Judaism nor Epicurus separated the human being into two parts – body and soul. Like the Jews, Epicurus thought of the human being as a unified, animated body. When the word *soul* is used in either tradition, the term refers to inner thoughts and feelings, which are of course connected to the physical brain. When a person dies, the whole person dies. In neither Judaism nor Epicureanism is there a separate soul that is immortal.

In the Hebrew scriptures death is often described as being asleep. There is nothing wrong with a deep sleep. The dead are "resting in peace." In Judaism, the only remaining issue is whether their Jewish ancestors will be raised from the dead when the Messiah arrives to usher in the period of peace and harmony for the land of Israel. The Jews did not want their ancestors who had suffered in difficult times to miss out on the joy and happiness of living in the new life God would establish through the Messiah. Some Jews believed that when the Messiah came, their dead ancestors would be resurrected to return to enjoy life in the new world. Other Jews did not believe it was possible to resurrect a dead body. Let the dead continue to "rest in peace."

Both views can be found in the Hebrew scriptures. In Jesus' day, among the Jewish leaders, it was the Sadducees who denied the concept that the dead would be resurrected. The Pharisees, on the other hand, accepted the doctrine, excluding only certain apostates from the privilege of resurrection.

As a Jew, Jesus would have been aware of the traditional Jewish worldview that death is the completion of life. His familiarity with Epicureanism would also lead him to the same understanding.

Did Jesus believe in an eternal life after death? The first thing to note is there are no teachings of his to answer the question. In any event, when it comes to the matter of death and what happens after death, there is no evidence Jesus departed from the teachings of Judaism or Epicureanism. If the major issue of our human existence on this earth had been, "Where will I spend eternity?" Jesus certainly would have made that issue a priority in his teachings. In Mark, Matthew, and Luke, Jesus does not say anything about eternity and where one might spend it.

We do know Jesus did not threaten punishment after death, nor did he offer a reward in some afterlife. He did not use the threat of hell as a weapon to frighten people into following him, nor did he offer a hope for immortality after death. His entire approach was to deal with the life we have on this earth.

The following parable Jesus told confirms this as his focus:

> *There was a rich man whose fields produced a bumper crop. He asks, "What do I do now since I don't have any place to store my crops? I know!" he says, "I'll tear down my barns and build larger ones so I can store all my grain and my goods. Then I'll say to myself, 'You have plenty put away for years to come. Take it easy, eat, drink, and enjoy yourself.'" But God said to him, "You fool! This night your life will be demanded back from you. All this stuff you've collected— whose will it be now.* (Luke 12:16-20)

Notice, God does not threaten the man with any punishment after he dies. God calls the man a fool because he has made it his top priority to build bigger barns to store his goods. God then simply states that the man will die, and someone else will get the benefit of all his efforts. If the issue had been where the man would spend eternity, this would have been a great opportunity for Jesus to end the parable with some words about life after death.

Epicurus, in his effort to dispel the fear of death and punishment after death, dealt with the subject thoroughly. According to Epicurus, the first step in dealing with death is to face the reality of death. Humans are part of the animal kingdom, and like all animals, each human person will die. One of Epicurus' disciples, Metrodorus, penned these words on behalf of the master: *Against all else it is possible to establish security, but as for death, human beings inhabit a city without walls.*

Epicurus expands on this teaching with these words:

> *Habituate yourself to the thought that death is nothing to us, because all good and evil lie in consciousness and death is the loss of consciousness. Consequently, a right understanding of the fact that death means nothing to us renders enjoyable the mortality of life, not by the addition of infinite time but by taking away the yearning for immortality. For there is nothing to fear in living for the man who has thoroughly grasped the idea that there is nothing to fear in not living.*

Epicurus taught that victory over the fear of death can be achieved by the person who has carefully reasoned the issue of death and who reflects that he has enjoyed the fullness of happiness in this life. The disciple Metrodorus expressed the victory with these words:

> *When necessity calls upon us to depart, spitting lustily upon life and upon those who madly cling to it, we shall take our leave of living with a glorious paean of victory, hymning the refrain that we have lived the good life.*

Epicurus and Jesus dealt with the fear of death by reassuring their followers that nothing bad can happen to them after death. There is no need to have a fear of death or what happens after we die. The important reality about which we can be certain is that we have this one life here on earth, and it is in this life we have the opportunity to find fulfillment and happiness.

CHAPTER THIRTY

The Art of Making Choices

Every day we make hundreds of decisions. Some are small and trivial; others are dramatic and life changing. Both Epicurus and Jesus offer guidance about the important issue of decision-making.

Epicurus says,

> *To all desires must be applied this question: What will be the result for me if the object of this desire is attained and what if it is not?"*

Epicurus calls this decision-making process the Calculus of Advantage. The individual should calculate the advantages and disadvantages of a certain action and seek to make the best decision in each situation. He describes it this way:

> *Nature provides that life is made pleasant by sober contemplation and by close examination of the reasons for deciding to take or not take any particular action.*
>
> *The proper procedure in all actions is to scan the advantages and disadvantages and weigh them against each other.*

He continues:

> *Human nature is not to be coerced but persuaded, and we shall persuade her by satisfying the necessary desires and the natural desires if they are not injurious, but relentlessly denying the harmful.*

Epicurus teaches that sometimes we deliberately choose to endure temporary pain for the subsequent pleasure that outweighs the pain.

> It is conducive to health; it enables the individual to face unflinching the vicissitudes of life; it disposes men to exercise better judgment when rich foods become available after intervals of scarcity; lastly, it renders men dauntless in the face of Fortune.

Epicurus was the first Greek philosopher to exalt the concept of the freedom of choice, what today we call free will. He taught that this concept is not purely selfish because it involves considering the effects of our decisions on others. In this regard, Jesus notes that there are two Great Commandments. One of them is *Love God"* "and the other is *"Love your neighbor as yourself."* In other words, consider the effect of your actions on others. This comes close to the Golden Rule, taught by Jesus and many other religious traditions: *Do unto others as you would have them do unto you.*

Jesus employs the Calculus of Advantage with the following bit of wisdom, found in Matthew 10:16:

> You must be as gentle as a dove and as sly as a snake.

Jesus may have been speaking with a twinkle in his eye as he advised humanity to combine the seemingly contradictory postures of a dove and a snake. It is, however, a perfectly accurate description of the Calculus of Advantage. By being gentle toward others while using sly wisdom in decision-making, one can live a fulfilling and happy life.

Jesus also gave the following practical advice to the peasant villagers:

> When you are about to appear with your opponent before the magistrate, do your best to settle with him on the way or else he may drag you up before the judge, and the judge will turn you over to the jailer, and the jailer throw you into

prison. I tell you, you'll never get out of there until you have paid every last cent. (Luke 12:57-59)

Jesus is teaching his audience to use the Calculus of Advantage in an unpleasant situation. The peasants were often in debt to the wealthier members of society. When a peasant was unable to repay the debt, the one to whom the debt is owed would threaten to take him to court. The courts of that time were notorious for being unfair to the poor. The wealthy could simply bribe the judge and get the case settled in their favor. Jesus gave the sensible advice to try to settle out of court. It was the wise step to take, using the Calculus of Advantage.

The art of making choices is an essential aspect of a life of happiness and living well.

RE-IMAGINING A NEW LIFE AND A NEW WORLD

Jesus, the Jewish teacher and guide, and Epicurus, the Greek philosopher, laid out a sensible path for creating a meaningful, happy, and fulfilling life by being loving and compassionate. Through the twists and turns of history their teachings were lost and/or rejected by the dominating Christian leadership in Europe. However, first through the Renaissance and then through the Enlightenment, the wisdom of these two great figures is now available to us. In addition, the recent studies of the Science of Happiness have confirmed and enhanced the wisdom of these two masters from antiquity.

Using their combined wisdom, we can live a fulfilling and happy life, and we can make a difference in this world. As American journalist and social activist Dorothy Day wrote,

> *We can throw one pebble in the pond and be confident that its ever-widening circle will reach around the world.*

The most worthwhile action we can take is to try to put happiness into the lives of others. Every time you bring happiness to another, you are dropping a pebble into the pond and making the world a better place.

The great orator of the latter part of the 19th century, Robert Ingersoll, wisely wrote:

> *The way to be happy is to make others so.*

You can start where you are. Each act of loving kindness can bring happiness to others in your neighborhood and can extend, in an ever-widening circle, around the world. Your life matters!

We can change the world, even as we ourselves are changed. We can work toward a more just and compassionate community, state, nation, and world.

It is all too easy to let a sense of worthlessness pervade our existence. We may feel our small acts of kindness will not make any difference. Keep in mind, though, these words from the pen of Charles Dickens:

No one is useless in this world who lightens the burden of another.

The teller of fables, Aesop, put it this way:

No act of kindness, no matter how small, is ever wasted.

America was founded upon the Epicurean principle of happiness: As one of our founders, John Adams, expressed it:

The happiness of society is the end (goal) of society.

Jeremy Bentham, English philosopher, jurist, and social reformer, established this principle, which had a strong influence on the founders of America:

It is the greatest happiness of the greatest number that is the measure of right and wrong.

The way to make America a healthier, safer nation, is to work toward spreading happiness to all our citizens. Happy people make better citizens. Happy people commit less crime and make for a safer nation. Happy people make better health decisions, thus helping create a healthier nation.

Perhaps English philosopher and sociologist Herbert Spencer said it best:

No one can be perfectly happy until all are happy.

What can you do to bring more happiness into our world, especially to those most in need? Epicurus and Jesus provide the answer, confirmed by the Science of Happiness. Follow their wisdom and live a life of wellbeing and happiness.

188

APPENDIX A

The Teachings of Jesus of Nazareth

Sayings Considered by the Jesus Seminar to Have Originated

with Jesus of Nazareth

1. Original Sayings Found in the Gospel of Luke:

Prophet without Honor	4:24
Wine and Wineskins	5:37-39
Blessings on You Poor	6:20
Blessings on You Hungry	6:22
Love Your Enemies	6:27, 35
Turn the Other Cheek	6:29
Coat and Shirt	6:29
Give to Beggars	6:30
No Merit in Loving Those Who Love You	6:32
Lend without Return	6:34-35
The Compassion of God	6:36

Do not Judge	6:37
Forgive and You Will Be Forgiven	6:37
Speck and Log	6:41-42
Grapes, Thorns, Figs, and Thistles	6:43-45
John the Baptist in the Wilderness	7:24-25
Hidden and Revealed	8:17
To Have and Have Not	8:18
Nowhere to Lay His Head	9:58
Let the Dead Bury the Dead	9:60
Stay at One House	10:7
Entering a Town	10:8
Eat What Is Served	10:8-9
Satan Falls Like Lightning	10:18
Parable: The Good Samaritan	10:30-35
The Peasants' Prayer (the Lord's Prayer)	11:2-4
Parable: The Friend at Midnight	11:5-8
Seek and Find	11:9
Seek and Knock	11:9-10
Government and House Divided	11:17
Satan Divided	11:18-19
By the Finger of God	11:20
A Strong Man	11:21-22

Parable: The Lost Coin	15:8-10
Parable: The Prodigal Son	15:11-32
Parable: The Shrewd Manager	16:1-8a
Serving Two Masters	16:13
Coming of the Kingdom	17:20-21
Saving One's Life	17:33
Parable: The Widow and the Judge	18:2-8
Parable: The Pharisee and the Tax Collector	18:9-14
Parable: Money Held in Trust	19:12-24
Be on Guard against Prideful Scholars	20:45-46

2. Original Sayings Found Only in Matthew

City on a Mountain	5:14
Sun and Rain on the Just and the Unjust	5:45
Left Hand and Right Hand	6:3
Sly as a Snake	10:16
Parable: Treasure in the Field	13:44
Parable: The Precious Pearl	13:45-46
Parable: The Unforgiving Slave	18:23-35
Castration for Heaven	19:11-12
Parable: The Vineyard Laborers	20:1-15
First and Last	20:16

3. Original Sayings Found Only in Mark

Healthy Do Not Need a Doctor	2:17
Fasting and Wedding	2:19
Lord of the Sabbath	2:27-28
Parable: Sower and the Seeds	4:3-8
Parable: The Seed and the Harvest	4:26-29
Prophet without Honor	5:4
What Defiles a Person	7:14-15
Children in the Kingdom	10:14
Difficult for the Rich	10:23
Camel and Eye of the Needle	10:25
Parable: The Leased Vineyard	12:1-8
True Relatives	12:33-35

4. Original Sayings Found Only in the Gospel of Thomas

The Rich Investor (63:1-3)

There was a rich person who had a great deal of money. He said, "I shall invest my money so that I may sow, reap, plant, and fill my storehouses with produce, that I may lack nothing." These were the things he was thinking in his heart, but that very night he died.

The Empty Jar (97)

The [Father's] imperial rule is like a woman who was carrying a jar full of meal. While she was walking along a distant road, the handle of the jar broke and the meal spilled behind her along the road. She didn't know it: she hadn't noticed a problem. When she reached her house, she put the jar down and discovered it was empty.

The Assassin (98)

The Father's imperial rule is like a person who wanted to kill someone powerful. While still at home he drew his sword and thrust it into the wall to find out whether his hand would go in. Then he killed the powerful one.

APPENDIX B

Jesus and Ecclesiastes

Jesus was born into a Jewish family in the village of Nazareth, in the province of Galilee, in the nation of Israel, all occupied by Jews. Thus, Jesus was deeply immersed in the Jewish culture of that day. As a young boy he would have attended he local synagogue school. In a nation that valued education and learning, even a small village like Nazareth would have provided an educational opportunity for its children. Jesus would have learned the Hebrew scriptures, as well as the history and traditions of Israel.

The Hebrew scriptures Jesus would have studied (the Old Testament) were divided into three distinct sections:

1. The history of Israel and its God.

2. The Prophets of Israel.

3. The Hebrew Wisdom Tradition.

In the teachings of Jesus found in Mark, Matthew, and Luke, Jesus shows little interest in the history section of the Hebrew scriptures (Genesis through Esther). He was quite familiar with the prophets of Israel, especially the social prophets (Isaiah, Jeremiah, Ezekiel, Hosea, Amos, and Micah).

In his teachings, Jesus does show a profound knowledge of the wisdom tradition of Israel (Job, Proverbs, Ecclesiastes, Song of Solomon, and some of the Psalms). His words and deeds reveal Jesus to have been an observant student of the wisdom tradition of Israel.

The authors of the Jewish wisdom tradition present their teachings as lessons they considered to be necessary for living a happy, moral, and flourishing life. They do not speculate about the future, nor were they interested in an afterlife. They focused on this present life, as experienced by everyone.

The teachings of Jesus display a clear connection with the teachings of Ecclesiastes, who lived about two hundred years before Jesus. The theme of his writings is found in the opening verses of the book of Ecclesiastes:

> *There is nothing better for mortals than to eat and drink and find enjoyment in their toil.* (Ecclesiastes 1:20) See also 3:22, 5:18, 8:15. 9:7-9.

His message is clear. He recommends living a fulfilling and meaningful life by pursuing the activities in which one finds delight, including one's career.

There are certain themes Jesus held in common with Ecclesiastes. It is helpful to note these connections, as well as the differences between these two teachers.

First, both Ecclesiastes and Jesus saw the futility of seeking happiness and fulfillment from acquiring more wealth and accumulating more material goods. They indicate the pleasant and peaceful life arises from always acting morally and prudently. Happy people do not spend their time "chasing after the wind," an image Ecclesiastes uses to describe the futility of seeking happiness by trying to grasp more wealth and more goods.

Another characteristic they shared was the value of learning from nature. They both regarded nature as a great teacher. Ecclesiastes was a realist and encouraged people to be aware of the natural order of things, the way they are in this world. He advises people to look to the animals with whom we share this planet: we all share the same breath, the same basic needs, and the same ultimate fate – death. Jesus also taught people to learn from nature, how to live free from fretfulness about food or clothing, or even death.

Jesus had an affinity to Ecclesiastes in that they both emphasized living a simple life. Living simply, within one's means, frees one from worry and fear about the future, and is the foundation of a happy and fulfilling life.

Ecclesiastes and Jesus both dealt with issues of human life, issues common to all humanity. They were each concerned with the life of the individual person. Jesus, however, understood one essential truth Ecclesiastes seemed to lack, a truth borne out in numerous recent studies about living a good and meaningful life. In study after study it has been show that the key to a happy life is good social relationships. Jesus included in his teachings the importance of living in harmonious and compassionate relationships with one another. There is a social and political passion in Jesus we do not find in Ecclesiastes.

Both teachers thought deeply about the human life experience. As a realist, Ecclesiastes insisted we face up to the finiteness of the human condition, and the fact that life ends at death. Jesus never contradicted the basic facts of life and death that Ecclesiastes saw. They both acknowledged the reality that every human life is bittersweet, a mixture of pain and pleasure. While Ecclesiastes became melancholy about the human condition, Jesus taught humanity to face the future with trust and hope. Jesus offered a vision of what life can be when life is lived with a mutual care for one another.

BIBLIOGRAPHY

Barber, William J. II. *Forward Together,* Chalice Press, 2014.

Beeker, Detlef. *The 90-Day Happiness Journal,* Detlef Beeker, 2019.

Borg, Marcus. *Jesus: Uncovering the Life, Teachings, and Relevance of a Religious Revolutionary.* New York: Harper Collins, 2006.

_____. *Meeting Jesus Again for the First Time*, New York: HarperCollins, 1994.

Cahill, Thomas. *Heretics and Heroes,* New York: Doubleday, 2013.

Cahn, Stephen M., and Christine Vitrano. *Happiness and Goodness,* New York: Columbia University Press, 2015.

Chilton, Bruce. *Rabbi Jesus: An intimate Biography.* New York: Doubleday, 2000.

Chittister, Joan. *The Time is Now,* New York: Convergent Books, 2019.

Crespo, Hiram. *Tending the Epicurean Garden,* Washington, D.C.: Humanist Press, 2014.

Crossan, John Dominic. *The Birth of Christianity.* San Francisco: Harper San Francisco, 1998.

_____. *The Historical Jesus: The Life of a Mediterranean Jewish Peasant*, San Francisco: Harper San Francisco, 1991.

DeWitt, Norman Wentworth. *Epicurus and His Philosophy,* St. Paul, Minnesota: University of Minnesota Press, 1954.

_____. *St. Paul and Epicurus,* St. Paul, Minnesota: University of Minnesota Press, 1954.

Dunn, Elizabeth and Norton, Michael. *Happy Money,* New York: Simon & Schuster, 2013.

Ellerbe, Helen, *The Dark Side of Christian History,* Morningstar Books: San Rafael, California, 1995.

Epicurus. *The Art of Happiness,* translated by George K. Strodach, New York: Penguin Books, 2012.

Fox, Matthew. *A Spirituality Name Compassion,* New York: HarperCollins, 1979.

Funk, Robert W. *A Credible Jesus: Fragments of a Vision.* Santa Rosa, CA: Polebridge Press, 2002.

_____. *Honest to Jesus: Jesus for a New Millennium.* San Francisco: Harper San Francisco, 1996.

Funk, Robert W., Roy W. Hoover, and the Jesus Seminar. *The Five Gospels: The Search for the Authentic Words of Jesus.* Santa Rosa, CA: Polebridge Press, 1993.

Funk, Robert W., and The Jesus Seminar. *The Acts of Jesus: What Did Jesus Really Do?* Santa Rosa, CA: Polebridge Press, 1998.

Galston, David. *Embracing the Human Jesus,* Santa Rosa, CA: Polebridge Press, 2012.

Gilbert, Daniel. Stumbling on Happiness, New York: Random House, Inc., 2016.

Gordan, Dane R. and David B. Suits, eds. *Epicurus: His Continuing Influences and Contemporary Relevance,* Rochester New York: Cary Graphic Arts Press, 2003.

Greenblat, Stephan. *The Swerve: How the World Became Modern,* New York: W. W. Norton and Company, 2011.

Hagenston, Richard. *Fabricating Faith,* Salem, Oregon: Polebridge Press, 2014.

Harris, Russ. *The Happiness Trap,* Boulder, Colorado: Trumpeter Books, 2007.

Hedrick, Charles W. *The Wisdom of Jesus.* Cascade Books: Eugene, OR., 2014.

Horsley, Richard A. *Jesus and Empire: The Kingdom of God and the New World Disorder.* Minneapolis: Fortress, 1997.

BIBLIOGRAPHY

Isbouts, Jean-Pierre. *Young Jesus.* New York: Sterling Publish Company, 2008.

Jacoby, Susan. *Freethinkers,* New York: Henry Holt and Company, 2004.

Jones, Howard *The Epicurean Tradition,* London: Routledge, 1989.

Klein, Daniel. *Travels with Epicurus,* New York: Penguin Books, 2012.

Korten, David C. *The Great Turning,* San Francisco: Berrett-Kohler, 2006.

Laughlin, Paul Allen. *Remedial Christianity.* Santa Rosa, CA: Polebridge Press, 2000.

Lee, Ingrid Fetell. *Joyful,* New York: Hachette Book Group, 2018.

Kloppenborg, John S. *Q Thomas Reader.* Santa Rosa, CA: Polebridge Press, 1990.

Mack, Burton. *The Lost Gospel: The Book of Q and Christian Origins.* San Francisco: HarperSanFrancisco, 1993.

Manchester, William. *A World Lit Only by Fire,* New York: Little, Brown, & Company, 1992.

Myers, David G. *The Pursuit of Happiness,* New York: Harper Collins, 1992.

Meyers, Robin R., *Saving Jesus from the Church,* New York: Harper Collins, 2009.

Miller, Robert J., ed. *The Complete Gospels.* Santa Rosa, CA: Polebridge Press, 1992.

Mills, Stephanie, *Epicurean Simplicity,* Washington, D. C.: Island Press, 2002.

Mitchell, Stephen. *The Gospel According to Jesus.* New York: HarperCollins, 1991.

Moore, Thomas. *Writing in the Sand,* Carlsbad, California: Hay House, Inc. 2009.

O'Connor, Eugene. *The Essential Jesus,* New York: Prometheus Books, 1993.

O'Dell Donald L. *How the Bible became the Bible*, 2nd Ed., Donald L. O'Dell, 2019.

Pinker, Steven. *Enlightenment Now,* New York: Penguin Random House, 2020.

Robinson, James M. *The Gospel of Jesus: In Search of the Original Good News,* New York: HarperCollins, 2005.

Salzberg, Sharon. *Lovingkindness,* Boulder, Colorado: Shambhala Publications, 1995.

Salzgeber, Nils. *The Happy Life Formula,* Nils Salzgeber, 2018.

Scott, Bernard Brandon. *The Real Paul,* Salem, OR: Polebridge Press, 2015.

Sheehan, Thomas. *The First Coming: How the Kingdom of God Became Christianity*, New York: Vintage Books.

Shi, David E. *The Simple Life,* Athens, Georgia: The University of Georgia Press, 1985.

Shimoff, Marci. *Happy for No Reason,* New York: Atria Books, 2009.

Spong, John Shelby. *Jesus for the Nonreligious,* San Francisco: Harper San Francisco, 2007.

_____. *Why Christianity Must Change or Die,* San Francisco: Harper San Francisco, 1998.

Stewart, Matthew, *Nature's God,* New York: W. W. Norton & Company, 2014.

Taussig, Hal. *Jesus Before God: The Prayer Life of the Historical Jesus,* Santa Rosa, CA: Polebridge Press, 1999.

Tolle, Eckhart, *The Power of Now,* Novato, California: New World Library, 1999.

Tutu, Desmond and Dalai Lama, *The Book of Joy,* New York: Penguin Random House, 2016

Vermes, Geza, *Jesus the Jew,* New York: Macmillan Publishing Company, 1973.

White, L. Michael, *From Jesus to Christianity,* San Francisco: Harper San Francisco, 2004.

Wilson, Catherine, *Epicureanism at the Origins of Modernity,* Oxford: Clarendon Press, 2008.

BIBLIOGRAPHY

_____ . *How to be an Epicurean,* New York: Basic Books, 2019.

Wright, Jerry R., *Reimaging God and Religion,* Asheville, North Carolina: Chiron Publications, 2018.

Ziegler, Hamish W. *The Happy People of Asheville: What Makes a Happy Town,* Asheville, NC: Hamish W. Ziegler, 2016.

Made in the USA
Monee, IL
30 March 2021